The Episcopal Handbook

The Episcopal Handbook

 Morehouse Publishing

THE EPISCOPAL HANDBOOK

Part of this book was originally published as the Lutheran Handbook © 2005, Augsburg Fortress.

Elements of Worst-Case Scenario Survival Handbook ® trade dress have been used with permission of and under license from Quirk Productions, Inc. Based on the trade dress of The Worst-Case Scenario Survival Handbook Series, by Joshua Piven and David Borgenicht, published by Chronicle Books, LLC. Worst-Case Scenario ® and The Worst-Case Scenario Survival Handbook Series ® are registered trademarks of Quirk Productions, Inc., 215 Church Street, Philadelphia, PA 19106.

Scripture quotations are from the New Revised Standard Version Bible, copyright © 1989, Division of Christian Education of the National Council of the Churches of Christ in the United States of America. Used by permission. All rights reserved.

Pages 211–225: Glossary adapted from *Altar Guild and Sacristy Handbook,* by S. Anita Stauffer, copyright © 2000 Augsburg Fortress; also adapted from *Words of Our Worship: A Practical Liturgical Dictionary* by Charles Mortimer Guilbert, copyright © 1988 Church Hymnal Corporation; and from The Book of Common Prayer.

New brand development editor: Kristofer Skrade
Editors: Barbara S. Wilson and Arlene Flancher; Susan Erdey
Production editors: Linnea Fitzpatrick, James Satter, Eileen Engebretson, and Josh Messner
Interior illustrator: Brenda Brown, Dorothy Thompson Perez
Interior layout: John Eagleson

Contributing writers: Rod Anderson, Chip Borgstadt, Ramona S. Bouzard, Walter C. Bouzard, Eric Burtness, Louis R. Carlozo, Carol Carver, Chris Duckworth, Susan T. Erdey, Rod Hank, Paul N. Hanson, Susan Houglum, Mark J. Jackson, Rolf A. Jacobson, Mark D. Johns, Mark K. Johnson, Ken Sundet Jones, James Kasperson, Timothy Keyl, Charles R. Lane, Susan M. Lang, Catherine Malotky, Mark C. Mattes, Sally Messner, Jennifer Moland-Kovash, Seth Moland-Kovash, Jan Nunley, Paul Owens, Rebecca Ninke, Marc Ostlie-Olson, Frank L. Tedeschi, Tom Teichmann, Megan J. Thorvilson, Megan Torgerson, Erik Ullestad, Darin Wiebe, Hans Wiersma, Chris Yaw, and Steven Zittergruen

ISBN 978-0-8192-2329-6

The paper used in this publication meets the minimum requirements of American National Standard for Information Sciences–Permanence of Paper for Printed Library Materials, ANSI Z329.48-1984.

Manufactured in Canada

12   11   4   5   6   7   8   9   10

CONTENTS

Bible Stuff 149

Maps, Diagrams, Charts, and Glossary 189

BRIEF EXPLANATION OF THE EPISCOPAL SHIELD

The Episcopal Church shield is a familiar symbol found on signs and in newspaper ads in cities and towns throughout the United States, usually accompanied by the words, "The Episcopal Church Welcomes You," together with information about a local church's location and worship schedule.

The shield and its corresponding Episcopal Church flag were officially adopted by the General Convention of 1940 and are rich in symbolism. The shield is usually presented in red, white, and blue (see cover). The red cross on a white field is an ancient Christian symbol, white representing the purity of Jesus and red representing his sacrifice on the cross and the blood of Christian martyrs. The red cross is also known as the cross of St. George, patron saint of England, and indicates the Episcopal Church's descent from the Church of England. The blue field in the upper left is the color traditionally associated with the Blessed Virgin Mary and is symbolic of Jesus' human nature, which he received from his mother. The X-shaped cross is the cross of St. Andrew, patron saint of Scotland, and recalls the Episcopal Church's indebtedness to the Scottish Episcopal Church for the consecration of its first bishop, Samuel Seabury, as Bishop of Connecticut in 1784. The St. Andrew's cross is made up of nine smaller cross-crosslets that represent the nine original American dioceses which met in Philadelphia in 1789 to adopt the constitution of the Episcopal Church.

They are: Connecticut (established in 1783), Maryland (1783), Massachusetts (1784), Pennsylvania (1784), New Jersey (1785), New York (1785), South Carolina (1785), Virginia (1785), and Delaware (1786).

INTRODUCTION

Just before the turn of the millennium, a small, yellow paperback appeared on the shelves and check-out counters of bookstores and hip, urban retailers. *The Worst Case Scenario Survival Handbook* showed the world how to live through earthquakes, fend off sharks, and stay alive in quicksand. Its frank demeanor, adventuresome spirit, and naked sincerity struck a chord with a nervous Y2K populace preoccupied with preparation. The book was a huge hit, spawning numerous spin-offs (eventually including *The Worst Case Scenario Survival Handbook: Weddings*), a TV show, even a board game. There seemed to be no end to our curious appetite for instruction and guidance no matter how remote the possibility of real-life application.

We all like to be prepared.

This includes those of us who participate in more mundane (and hopefully safer) activities like attending Sunday services at an Episcopal church. The particularities of receiving communion or the intricacies of four-part choral harmony are understandably mystifying to the newcomer. Liturgical churches can be intimidating and even uninspiring when we don't know what's going on. We need "survival" lessons of our own. Granted, parallels between enduring a poorly crafted sermon and surviving quicksand is certainly stretching things, as this would fail to consider that one could actually enjoy floating in quicksand.

So in the spirit — if not in the letter — of survival handbooks, we have endeavored to outline, with minimal blather and nominal peril, the great joys and wonders of life in the Episcopal Church. These days we're an increasingly diverse collection of Christians from varied backgrounds (70 percent are converts) who come together around shared convictions about prayer, liturgy, church government, and — most importantly — the life and ministry of Jesus Christ. We're a place that welcomes random questions and eccentric personalities. We're a peculiar people whose spiritual arc bends more towards boundless hope and a reasonable faith than hardened surety and entrenched absolutism.

For 400 years, Episcopalians have found comfort, nurture, fellowship, and encouragement in our faith communities. And we believe the Almighty is not finished with us yet. We believe — now more than ever — we provide a uniquely fulfilling and vital role in the panoply of modern Christian experiences on offer.

The pages that follow are abbreviated invitations to much longer conversations that can be continued with further reading via online and book resources or by visiting one of your 7,200 or so friendly neighborhood Episcopal congregations. We have chosen to write in a light-hearted manner, not so much due to market research, but because it comes so naturally to us. Episcopalians laugh a lot. This is a healthy response to our colorful heritage — and the endless evidence of God's continued hand upon such a flawed and faulty vessel. How else does one respond to our past — which includes a king who adored marriage as much as Elizabeth Taylor?

Our goal is to extend to Episcopalians and non-Episcopalians alike a generous invitation to learn more about our particular expression of the Christian faith. The Gospel of Jesus Christ as understood by Episcopalians isn't for everyone, but it is for us, and it may be for you, especially if you've read this far.

So relax, strap on your safety belt, and prepare for possibility over peril, imagination over anxiety, and dreams over danger. If the Christian life is the greatest adventure human life has to offer, why not pack a survival handbook?

CHURCH STUFF

HOW TO SURVIVE A BAPTISM

We start with baptism because this is the sacrament of beginnings.

Episcopalians understand baptism as full initiation into Christ's body, the Church, which is why we start early — with infants. Here's how one works:

Most baptisms are performed in churches where priests or bishops preside. But in an emergency, any baptized person can baptize.

The essence of the ceremony boils down to one sentence: "I baptize you in the name of the Father, and of the Son, and of the Holy Spirit."

The role of sponsors and godparents is to support those being baptized and to make promises on behalf of children. The whole congregation also joins in on these promises and pledges their support.

Typically, a baptismal candle is lit and presented to show the newly baptized person has received the light of Christ. It's appropriate to light these candles annually, on one's baptismal anniversary.

After baptism in water, the priest or bishop traces the cross on the baptized person's forehead, often with anointing oil (called "chrism") and declares that he or she is marked and sealed as Christ's own forever.

The basin that holds the water is typically called a font. Many of them have eight sides as a reminder of the "eighth day" — the day of circumcision for the Hebrews and a day of beginnings; the first day after seven.

Baptism is received by a believing heart that trusts in Christ. In the case of infant baptism, the baptized person "borrows" one from his or her parents and sponsors.

Water is an ancient symbol of cleansing and deliverance. The Lord uses it to wash away sins and make us new. Water itself can't do it, but it is the tangible symbol of the invisible power of God's forgiveness and acceptance.

Note: Episcopalians baptize people of all ages — not just infants.

HOW TO RECEIVE COMMUNION

The Sacrament of Holy Communion (also called the Holy Eucharist, or sometimes the Lord's Supper) is a central event in Episcopal worship. All five senses are engaged in communion, and it is the most interactive part of the service. Local customs for receiving communion can be confusing or complex, so it's wise to pay attention and prepare.

1 Determine which method of distribution is used.
Verbal directions or printed instructions will likely be given prior to the distribution. The most common methods for communion are the common cup and intinction.

Note: Some congregations commune at "tables" (gathered around the altar), and some practice "continuous communion" with bread and wine stations, and some do both.

2 Look for guidance from the usher.
The usher will direct the people in each row or pew to stand and get in line.

3 Proceed to the communion station.
Best practice is often simply to follow the person in front of you and do what they do.

4 Kneel, if appropriate.
Congregations that commune at "tables" often do so by instructing communicants to kneel at an altar railing. When this happens, remember to stand slowly to avoid jostling your neighbor. Assist people who are elderly with altar rail navigation when they need help.

Common Cup

❶ Receive the bread.

> *To receive the bread, make a "cross" or "cradle" with your hand, palms up.*

Extend your hands with palms facing up. After the celebrant places the bread in your open hands, grasp the piece with the fingers of one hand. When the server says, "The body of Christ, the Bread of Heaven," eat the bread.

Note: Bread is commonly distributed in both baked or "loaf" form and in wafer form. Either is acceptable.

❷ Receive the wine.

The wine will be served in a large cup or "chalice," as a sign of unity. Assist the celebrant by placing one hand underneath the cup and the other hand on its side. Help the server guide the chalice to your lips.

❸ Avoid leaving backwash.

Drink only one sip from the chalice. Remove your lips from the cup immediately after receiving the wine.

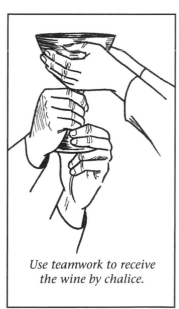

Use teamwork to receive the wine by chalice.

Intinction

Note: The word *intinction* is from the Latin word *intingere*, which means "to dip."

❶ Receive the bread.
Follow the same procedure as with the chalice, but DO NOT EAT THE BREAD YET. If you accidentally eat the bread prematurely, REMAIN CALM. Simply ask for another piece.

Gently dip the bread in the wine for communion by intinction.

❷ Receive the wine.
Position the bread you are holding over the chalice. Grasp the bread tightly and dip just the edge of it into the wine. When the server says, "The Blood of Christ, the cup of salvation," eat the wine-soaked bread.

❸ Do not panic if you accidentally drop your bread into the chalice.
Again, the server can provide you with more bread. If the person distributing bread is too far away, the chalice bearer may allow you to drink directly from the cup. Receiving only one element (bread or wine) counts as full participation in communion.

Once You Have Communed

◆ *Return to your seat.* If communion is distributed in one continuous line, you may immediately return to your pew.

   OR

◆ *Wait for the completion of the distribution.* If you're being served as a group at the altar rail, you may need to wait until all other worshipers are served before returning to your seat. This is an appropriate time to close your eyes, pray, or listen to the communion music.

◆ Continue to participate when seated. After returning to your place, you may join the congregation in singing the remaining communion hymns, or pray in silence.

Be Aware

◆ When receiving the bread, place one upward palm on top of the other symbolically to make a "cross" or "cradle" with your hands.

◆ Some congregations offer the option of non-alcoholic wine in addition to wine during communion. Verbal or written instructions will be given prior to distribution so you will be able to identify which chalice or cup contains alcohol-free wine.

◆ After receiving the bread and wine, avoid saying, "Thank you" to the server. The body and blood are gifts from God. If you wish, a gentle "Amen" is appropriate.

◆ Pastoral blessings are often available for children or adults who are not communing. Simply cross your arms over your chest if you wish to receive a blessing.

WHY YOU WON'T GET SICK SHARING A COMMUNION CUP

In this age of hand sanitizers, it may appear a bit unseemly for a whole church full of people to actually drink out of the same chalice. Won't I catch a cold or pass on the flu? Actually, sharing a common cup isn't as hazardous as one might suspect.

Most Episcopal churches use real wine — and then some; we use fortified wine such as port. This has a high alcohol content, killing off most every germ.

Not long ago a Canadian doctor named David Gould did research into illnesses passed through a common cup and found churchgoers more likely to get sick from airborne infections than from a shared chalice. "If communion cups were a danger there would be cases of mass infections," he wrote, and there aren't.

However, if you still feel uncomfortable drinking the wine (or are a recovering alcoholic), this is not essential to receiving Christ at Communion. Episcopalians believe Christ is equally present in both the consecrated bread and the wine, so receiving one, the other, or both, gets you no more (or less) of Christ's presence.

HOW TO SING A HYMN (AND WHY YOU MIGHT WANT TO)

Music is an important part of the Episcopal tradition and an enjoyable way to build community. (See page 108 for "Ten Famous Hymns Written by Episcopalians or Anglicans.") Hymn singing can be done without demonstrable emotion, but many otherwise prim and proper Episcopalians appropriately channel emotion into their hymn singing and are therefore loud.

❶ Locate hymns in advance.
As you prepare for worship, consult the worship bulletin or the hymn board to find numbers for the day's hymns. Bookmark these pages in the hymnal using an offering envelope or bulletin insert.

❷ Familiarize yourself with the hymns.
Examine the composer credits, the years the composer(s) lived, and whether the tune has a different name than the hymn itself. Note how the hymn is categorized in the hymnal. The Hymnal 1982 groups the songs into categories, such as "Holy Eucharist" and "Christmas."

❸ Assist nearby visitors or children.
Using a hymnal can be confusing. If your neighbor seems disoriented, help them find the correct pages, or let them read from your book.

❹ Adopt a posture for best vocal performance.
Hold the hymnal away from your body at chest level.
Place one hand under the spine of the binding, leaving
the other hand free to turn the pages. Keep your chin
up so your voice projects outward.

❺ Begin singing.
If the hymn is un-
familiar, sing the
melody for the first
verse. If you read
music, explore the
written harmony parts
during the remaining
verses. Loud-singing
neighbors may or
may not be in tune,
so follow them with
caution.

*Support the hymnal's spine
with one hand. Place the other
on the open page.*

**❻ Focus on hymn's
content.**
Some of the lyrics may connect with a scripture reading
of the day. Certain ones may be especially inspiring.

❼ Avoid dreariness.
Hymns are often sung in such a serious way that the
congregation forgets to enjoy the music. Sing with
energy and feeling.

Be Aware

- Hymnals are not just for use at church. Consider keeping a personal copy of your congregation's hymnal at home for further reference and study. Hymnals also make excellent baptism or confirmation gifts.

- Some hymns use words and phrases that are difficult to understand (such as, "Here I raise my Ebenezer," from the hymn "Come Thou Fount of Every Blessing" in *Lift Every Voice and Sing II*). Use a dictionary or a Bible with a concordance to clear up any uncertainty.

HOW TO RESPOND WHEN SOMEONE SITS IN YOUR PEW

We all carry a bubble of personal space. For some people, it's several feet. For others, it's about a millimeter. Wherever on the spectrum you happen to fall, there are certain situations in which we invite visitors into our little sphere of experience — like at church. Furthermore, human beings are territorial in nature and sometimes see strangers inside the bubble as an affront. These situations need not be cause for alarm.

1 **Smile and greet the "intruders."**
Oftentimes they are visitors to your congregation — new blood. Avoid creating bad blood you might regret later on. Make solid eye contact so they know you mean it, shake hands with them, and leave no impression that they've done something wrong.

2 **View the "intrusion" as an opportunity.**
Remember, you don't own the pew; you just borrow it once a week. Take the opportunity to get out of your rut and sit someplace new. This will physically emphasize a change in your perspective and may yield new spiritual discoveries.

3 **If you can tell that your new friends feel uncomfortable at having displaced you, despite your efforts to the contrary, make an extra effort to welcome them.**
Consider taking them to brunch after church to become acquainted. If there are too many for you to foot the bill, consider inviting them to accompany you on a "go Dutch" basis. This will eliminate any hierarchy and place you on equal footing.

WHAT ARE ALL THOSE BOOKS IN THE PEW?

Episcopalians are a people of the book.

Actually, several books.

While the Bible is the foundation of our library, it is not the only book we rely on to help us worship. That's why you'll find several books in the pews of most Episcopal churches.

The most common (by far) is the 1979 edition of The Book of Common Prayer. Inside you'll find over 1,000 pages of some of the richest and most beautiful liturgies ever written. In addition to Sunday morning worship services, there are baptism, wedding, and funeral services, prayers, historical documents, and much more. It abounds in scriptural imagery and phraseology. We like to think of the Book of Common Prayer as the Bible rearranged for worship.

A second book is *The Hymnal 1982*. This includes a rich collection of more than 700 hymns. Some of these are more than one thousand years old. Others are just a few decades new. One thing they all have in common is that they're widely considered to be some of the best worship music that's ever been written — not just in the last twenty years, but in the last twenty centuries.

Other books you may find in the pews include Bibles and supplemental hymnbooks like *Lift Every Voice and Sing II* or *Wonder, Love and Praise*. You may also find visitors' brochures and the occasional coloring book (proof that not every Episcopalian knows how to read).

While some people consider written prayers and prescribed liturgy tedious and lacking spontaneity, it can also be said that writing things down is a rather high form of respect and sincerity. The meticulousness with which these books are written, edited, and arranged bespeaks the reverence, foresight, and values Episcopalians bring to their worship — even if this also means they have to bring their glasses.

WHY IS EVERYBODY KNEELING?

Subjects do it before kings, some men do it when proposing marriage, and Christians have historically done this when they go to church:

Kneeling.

It's an act of obeisance to authority, honor to royalty, and contrition for sin. It is one of three basic positions Episcopalians assume in the course of regular Sunday worship.

Typically, we kneel to confess our sins, to receive absolution, and to pray (although standing for prayer is an ancient and acceptable posture). Episcopalians kneel much less than we used to. It's not because we've gotten lazy, but in order to recover an ancient sensibility toward worship; the idea that Christianity is less about endless penitence than it is about continual rejoicing in the forgiveness Jesus brings.

So when we stand we do so to show respect, like during the reading of the Gospels, which are the four books that record the words and deeds of Jesus. We also stand to say the Creed, a 1,600-year-old statement of our beliefs. And we stand to sing. Not only does this help us sound better, but it also helps us express our thanksgiving and appreciation. Think standing ovation.

When we sit, we do so to convey our readiness to learn, like we (were supposed to) do at school. We sit to listen to the Old and New Testament lessons as well as the Psalm and the sermon.

Referred to by some as "pew aerobics," our penchant for communal participation comes from a shared belief that Sunday worship is not a spectator sport. Episcopalians are a liturgical church, the word liturgy meaning "work of the people." So kneeling, sitting, and standing are all about inspiring us to say thanks together, the very best way we know how.

WHY SOME EPISCOPALIANS BOW AND CROSS THEMSELVES (AND WHY SOME DON'T)

Roman Catholics and Latin American baseball players aren't the only ones. Many Episcopalians are also in the habit of practicing that ancient body prayer of crossing themselves. This is typically done when beginning and ending prayers and ceremonies. It's also a stand-alone practice of asking God to bless oneself.

To many Episcopalians, making the sign of the cross is a humble, silent prayer used to remind us of Christ's sacrifice and also the cross we are called to bear. Before Christ, the cross was an instrument of cruel punishment and a symbol of horror. After his sufferings, it became the sign of victory over evil and of life over death. Many people believe we do well to remind ourselves of this as often as possible.

Of course some Episcopalians don't agree. Some believe it's ostentatious and superfluous. Acts of worship are not primarily for ourselves, they're for God, so goes the argument, and the participation in outward signs of piety such as this should be avoided.

There are no hard and fast rules regarding body prayers in the Episcopal Church. Some people genuflect at the mention of the name of Jesus Christ, when approaching the altar, or when the processional cross goes by. Others don't. These are personal acts of piety and are completely optional. Bottom line: if it's for you, join in; if not, don't.

That said, here's how many Episcopalians cross themselves:

1. Touch the fingertips of your right hand to your forehead. Say "In the name of the Father..."

2. Touch your sternum. Say "and the Son..."

3. Touch the front side of your left shoulder. Say "And the Holy..."

4. Touch your right shoulder in roughly the same location. Say "Spirit."

5. Return your hand to your heart, or to your side, and say "Amen."

HOW TO SHARE THE PEACE

In Romans 16:16, Paul tells members of the congregation to "greet one another with a holy kiss." The First Letter of Peter ends, "Greet one another with a kiss of love. Peace to all of you who are in Christ" (1 Peter 5:14).

Some Episcopalians worry about this part of the worship service due to its free-for-all nature. Some also feel uncomfortable because of their fear of being hugged. You can survive the peace, however, with these steps.

❶ Adopt a peaceful frame of mind.
Clear your mind of distracting and disrupting thoughts so you can participate joyfully and reverently.

❷ Determine the appropriate form of safe touch.
Handshaking is most common. Be prepared, however, for hugs, half-hugs, one-armed hugs, pats, and other forms of physical contact. Nods are appropriate for distances greater than two pews or rows.

❸ Refrain from extraneous chitchat.
The sharing of the peace is not the time for lengthy introductions to new people, comments about the weather, or observations about yesterday's game. A brief encounter is appropriate, but save conversations for the coffee hour.

❹ Make appropriate eye contact.
Look the other person in the eye but do not stare. The action of looking the person in the eye highlights the relationship brothers and sisters in Christ have with one another.

Make good eye contact as you share God's peace with others.

❺ Declare the peace of God.
"The peace of the Lord be with you," "Peace be with
you," "The peace of God," "God's peace," and "The
peace of Christ," are ways of speaking the peace. Once
spoken, the peace is there. Move on to the next person.

Be Aware

◆ Safe touch involves contact that occurs within your
personal space but does not cause discomfort or unease.

WHAT IS THE BOOK OF COMMON PRAYER?

When King Henry VIII separated the Church of England from the authority of the Roman Catholic Church by the Act of Supremacy in 1534, it became necessary to revise the Church's worship to reflect the change.

The King told Archbishop Thomas Cranmer that he wanted all service books "newly examined, corrected, reformed, and castigated, from all manner of mention of the Bishop of Rome's name, from all apocryphas, feigned legends, superstitions, orations, collects, versicles, and responses; that the names and memories of all saints which be not mentioned in the Scripture or authentic doctors should be abolished, and put out of the same books and calendars, and that the service should be made out of the Scripture and other authentic doctors."

In 1544, Cranmer was ordered to prepare a general supplication "in our native English tongue," to be "continually from henceforth said and sung in all churches of our realm with such reverence and devotion as appertaineth." A new "Order of the Communion" passed Parliament in 1548, and the next year Parliament's "Act for Uniformity of Service and Administration of the Sacraments throughout the Realm" established "The Book of Common Prayer, and Administration of the Sacraments, and other rites and ceremonies of the Church, after the Use of the Church of England" as the official worship book for the Church.

The 1549 edition went through revisions in 1552 and 1559 before its present authorized form, the 1662 version, was finalized. It remains the official Book of Common Prayer for the Church of England.

Churches that trace their origin to the Church of England have usually revised and produced Prayer Books of their own to reflect their own national circumstances. The U.S. Episcopal Church separated from the Church of England in 1789 and published its first Book of Common Prayer, based on both the English and the Scottish prayer books. Thorough constitutional revisions to the American book have only been made in 1892, 1928, and 1979.

Each revision saw its own degree of controversy and opposition, although, as Cranmer himself said in the preface to the original: "There was never anything by the wit of man so well devised, or so sure established, which in continuance of time hath not been corrupted."

WHY DO EPISCOPALIANS READ THEIR PRAYERS?

When the disciples came to Jesus and asked him how they should pray, he didn't suggest that they make it up as they go along. He offered them a well thought out form of prayer that we call the "Our Father."

Episcopalians, like many Christians, believe that when we write our prayers down we carry forward an ancient tradition of order and structure suggested in Jesus' instructions to the disciples. After all, worship in Jesus' day was a highly structured affair, with written prayers for just about every occasion. One of the biggest collections still in use is the book of Psalms.

When we think about it, even the most laid-back, contemporary worship services rely on some written, pre-arranged format. There's the bulletin, the songs, and of course the sermon outline, if not the entire thing. Sure, there's the danger of written prayers becoming nothing more than hollow words and empty phrases, which is something Jesus warned against. However, written prayers have a lot to offer.

Episcopalians find that written prayers allow for common prayer. Our prayers allow us to partake more deeply in a shared experience of offering up something we agree on. Most of our prayers are pretty old and have stood the test of time regarding the beliefs they express and the clarity with which they state them. When we pray them we are uniting with generations of believers who have prayed the same prayers. Just think of the billions of people who have prayed popular written prayers like the Our Father, the Agnus Dei ("Lamb of God . . . ") or the Sanctus ("Holy, holy, holy . . . ").

Think of a written prayer as the refrain to your favorite song. That song may be several years old and you may have sung it hundreds of times. But that doesn't make it any less touching or enjoyable. Good songs age well, and so do good prayers.

HOW TO LISTEN TO A SERMON

Episcopalians believe God's Word comes to us through the sacraments and the preaching of Holy Scripture. Honoring God's Word, not to mention getting something out of church, includes diligent listening to the sermon and active mental participation.

1 Review active listening skills.
While the listener in this case doesn't get to speak, the sermon is still a conversation. Make mental notes as you listen. Take notice of where and why you react and which emotions you experience.

2 Take notes.
Note-taking promotes active listening and provides a good basis for later reflection. It also allows you to return to confusing or complicated parts at your own leisure. Some congregations provide space in the bulletin for notes, and some confirmation ministries provide structured worksheets.

3 Maintain good posture. Avoid slouching.
Sit upright with your feet planted firmly on the ground and your palms on your thighs. Beware of the impulse to slouch, cross your arms, or lean against your neighbor, as these can encourage drowsiness.

4 Listen for the gospel.
This will come in the form of a sentence most likely starting with the name Jesus and ending with the words *for you*. Upon hearing the gospel, you may feel a physical lightness, as though you've set down a great burden. You may cry tears of joy. This is normal.

❺ End by saying, "Amen."
Since preaching is mostly God's work, honor the Word by sealing the moment with this sacred word, which means, "It is most certainly true!"

❻ Review.
If you've taken written notes, read through them later that day or the next day and consider corresponding with the preacher if you have questions or need clarification. If you've taken mental notes, review them in a quiet moment. Consider sharing this review time with others in your congregation or household on a weekly basis.

HOW TO PASS THE PLATE

Passing the offering plate requires physical flexibility and an ability to adapt to differing practices. The offering is a practice that dates back to Old Testament times, linking money and personal finance directly to one's identity as a child of God. Giving of one's financial resources is an integral part of a healthy faith life.

❶ Pay close attention to instructions, if any.
The presiding minister may announce the method of offering, or instructions may be printed in the worship bulletin.

❷ Be alert for the plate's arrival at your row or pew.
Keep an eye on the ushers, if there are any. In most congregations, guiding and safeguarding the offering plate is their job, so wherever they are, so is the plate. As the plate approaches you, set aside other activity and prepare for passing.

❸ Avoid watching your neighbor or making judgments about their offering.
Many people contribute once a month by mail and some by automatic withdrawal from a bank account. If your neighbor passes the plate to you without placing an envelope, check, or cash in it, do not assume they didn't contribute.

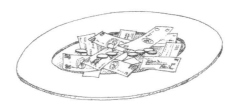

4 **Place your offering in the plate as you pass it politely to the next person.**
Do not attempt to make change from the plate if your offering is in cash. Avoid letting the plate rest in your lap as you finish writing a check. Simply pass it on and hand your check to an usher as you leave at the end of worship.

5 **Be sensitive to idiosyncrasies in plate types.**
Some congregations use traditional, wide-rimmed, felt-lined, brass-plated offering plates. Some use baskets of varying types. Some use cloth bags hung at the ends of long wooden poles that the ushers extend inward from the ends of the pews.

Be Aware

* Some congregations place the offering plate or basket at the rear of the worship space.

* Your church offering may be tax deductible, as provided by law. Consider making your offering by check or automatic withdrawal; you will receive a statement from your church in the first quarter of the next year.

* Churches often depend entirely upon the money that comes in through congregational offerings. If you are a member, resolve to work yourself toward tithing as a putting-your-money-where-your-mouth-is expression of faith. (The term tithing means "one-tenth" and refers to the practice of giving 10 percent of one's income to support the church's work.)

* Everyone, regardless of their age, has something to offer.

* Offerings are not fees or dues given out of obligation. They are gifts of thanksgiving returned to God from the heart.

HOW MUCH MONEY SHOULD I PUT INTO THE OFFERING PLATE?

As much (or as little) as you like.

Like most churches, Episcopal congregations exist mainly on donations from our members.

Once a year most parishes run a "stewardship" or "pledge campaign," asking each individual or family to make a financial promise for the upcoming year. We then total those promises and create our budget.

In general, Episcopal parishes spend the majority of their money on salaries, building upkeep, and programming and outreach. Since the first two tend to be fixed costs, the more money that is collected, the more a church's ministry can be expanded into new programs and help to those outside the parish.

Of course, donations also come in the form of volunteer time. For example, electricians help with maintenance and accountants help audit the books, which can be priceless.

However, the main reason for giving to a church has less to do with paying bills and much more to do with cultivating generous hearts. God wants you and me to be generous (2 Corinthians 9:7). The Lord wants us to be known not by the kind of car we drive, the size of the house we live in, or the jewelry we wear, but by our love. As Christ gave himself away for us, so too are we asked to give of ourselves away to others. So the old adage "give 'til it hurts" comes to mind — but, in fact, it could be better phrased as "give 'til it feels good."

That's why the Episcopal Church asks its members to use the tithe (10 percent of one's income) as a starting point. Tithing is never a requirement for membership; most parishes gratefully receive any contribution. However, money is a spiritual issue and our churches address it by gently challenging their members to grow — to strive less for acquiring things for ourselves, and doing more to help those in need.

Bottom line: when the plate gets passed, use your own discretion. Few people know (or care) how much money you put in. How much we give is between God and ourselves. But know that any contribution will be appreciated and, of course, tax deductible.

WHY IS THE ALTAR BIGGER THAN THE PULPIT (OR VICE VERSA)?

Church interiors offer more clues than a crime scene on a TV forensic drama.

Every banner, color, symbol, and piece of furniture gives us some sort of indication as to what goes on in that space, and what the people believe who call that space home. This is especially true when it comes to the size and placement of altars and pulpits in Episcopal churches.

Early Christian worship divided the Sunday service into two parts concentrating on Word and Sacrament. This continues today in Episcopal services (and others). That means during the first half of the service we hear Bible readings that usually include selections from the Old Testament, the Book of Psalms, the New Testament, and one of the Gospels. This is followed by a sermon.

The second half of the service revolves around the Sacrament of Communion. The celebrant prays a special prayer called the Eucharistic Prayer. And all focus is drawn to the altar and the symbol of Christ's sacrifice for us. The drama reaches a pinnacle when the bread is broken at the altar and offered to the people with the words, "The Gifts of God for the People of God."

Naturally, it is difficult to put equal weights on these two parts. Some congregations tend to be more protestant and put greater emphasis on the reading and exposition of the Bible — this explains congregations with large pulpits. Other congregations tend to be more catholic and are nurtured by the presence and mystery of Christ in the Eucharist. Thus, in addition to the presence of accessories like incense, bells, and ornate clergy dress, the altar is rather pronounced.

WHY IS THAT EMPTY CHAIR NEXT TO THE ALTAR?

No matter how full an Episcopal church may be on Sunday, chances are no one will be sitting in a sometimes ornate chair located somewhere near the altar.

This special seat is a sign and a symbol of the unity and authority that comes from the particular way Episcopalians have of organizing themselves: it's the bishop's chair.

The Episcopal Church believes in bishops, those experienced and talented among us who are called to lead the church. In fact, the word "Episcopal" means "bishop." Bishops are the head of a geographic area known as a diocese. In these dioceses are many parishes that a bishop oversees. He or she does this mainly through other clergy members, such as priests and deacons, who serve smaller geographic areas called parishes.

A bishop has one main seat; its Latin name is *cathedra*. This is where we get the word cathedral; literally, the place where the bishop is seated. However, bishops get out a lot, regularly visiting parishes, which is why we keep a seat for them. This is a reminder not only of the authority of the bishop, but of the bishop's prayers and presence with us. The empty chair, then, serves as a reminder for us to pray for our bishop as well.

TELLING THE SEASON OF THE YEAR BY THE COLOR OF THE ALTAR

Episcopal worship is color-coded.

Like other liturgical churches, the Episcopal Church upholds the long tradition of arranging the year around the life of Jesus Christ.

It all begins with Advent, the Christian New Year, which is a four-week countdown to Jesus' birthday, aka Christmas. We celebrate for 12 days before Epiphany (hence the famous carol, "On the first day of Christmas my true love gave to me . . . "). Epiphany commemorates the coming of the Three Kings and lasts until Ash Wednesday, aka the first day of Lent. Because Lent starts 40 days before Easter, the date is always different. That's because, as everybody knows, most Christians celebrate Easter on the first Sunday after the first full moon of the vernal equinox. (What, you didn't know that?) Lent leads us to Holy Week, and the Great Three Days, which culminates in Easter, the biggest holy day of them all, which is why we spend the next 50 days partying. Then we hit the day of Pentecost, the day the Holy Spirit came down on Jesus' disciples, and we're off on roughly seven months of studying the teachings and miracles of Jesus.

If you found this hard to follow, then you know why we've assigned colors to each season, which we display with banners on the walls, fabric on the pulpit, and, of course, the cloth on the altar.

THE SEASONS OF
THE CHURCH YEAR

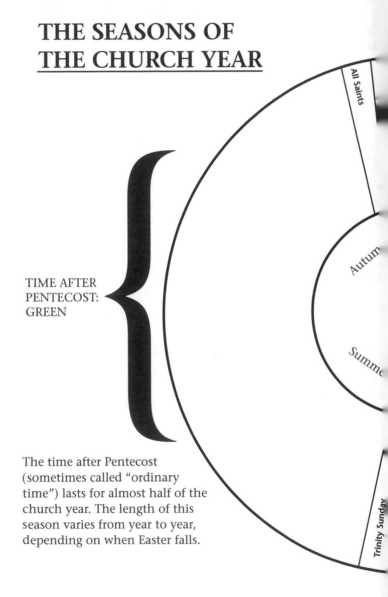

All Saints

Autumn

Summer

Trinity Sunday

TIME AFTER
PENTECOST:
GREEN

The time after Pentecost
(sometimes called "ordinary
time") lasts for almost half of the
church year. The length of this
season varies from year to year,
depending on when Easter falls.

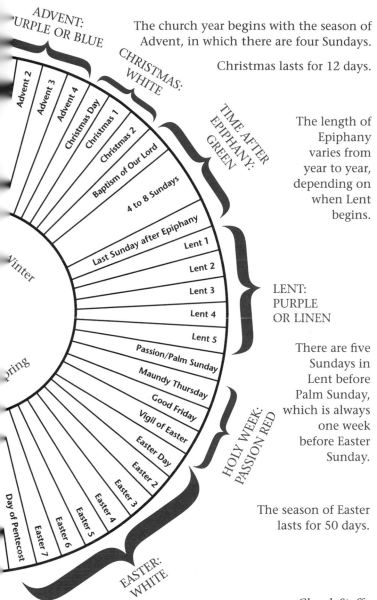

The church year begins with the season of Advent, in which there are four Sundays.

Christmas lasts for 12 days.

The length of Epiphany varies from year to year, depending on when Lent begins.

There are five Sundays in Lent before Palm Sunday, which is always one week before Easter Sunday.

The season of Easter lasts for 50 days.

ADVENT: PURPLE OR BLUE

CHRISTMAS: WHITE

TIME AFTER EPIPHANY: GREEN

LENT: PURPLE OR LINEN

HOLY WEEK: PASSION RED

EASTER: WHITE

Advent 2
Advent 3
Advent 4
Christmas Day
Christmas 1
Christmas 2
Baptism of Our Lord
4 to 8 Sundays
Last Sunday after Epiphany
Lent 1
Lent 2
Lent 3
Lent 4
Lent 5
Passion/Palm Sunday
Maundy Thursday
Good Friday
Vigil of Easter
Easter Day
Easter 2
Easter 3
Easter 4
Easter 5
Easter 6
Easter 7
Day of Pentecost

Winter

Spring

WHY ALL THE STAINED GLASS?

Formed by two of the world's most basic elements, sand and fire, it is no wonder that Christians have long seen glass in churches as a window to more than just the outside.

No one knows who invented stained glass (it may have started with jewelry) but its popularity began spreading in the Middle Ages during the European church and cathedral building boom. Advances in architecture allowed for large, sweeping windows and many church designers used them to say something big about God. Medieval craftsmen believed they were building sacred dwelling places for an all-powerful God. They were interested in creating an atmosphere of grandeur where people could really sense God's presence. Thus, early stained glass windows were to be experienced more than read.

Because stained glass in churches usually depicts a biblical scene, a sacrament, or the life of a famous saint, another big reason for its popularity is its effectiveness as a teaching tool. Think of stained glass windows as the medieval church's PowerPoint. They helped new Christians learn Bible stories and reminded older members of their sacred story.

The idea behind stained glass, and many furnishings in Episcopal churches, is that the presence of beautiful objects can lift our souls closer to God. Like nature, stained glass windows open our eyes to the wonders of God. They remind us of our past and point us to the future. When we look at stained glass we see God's story played out in myriad different levels. And when we think about it, that's really not a bad way to look out at the world.

DO EPISCOPALIANS BELIEVE IN SAINTS?

Of course they do. As with most things Episcopalian, however, it depends on how you define "believe" and "saints." All Christians are part of the Communion of Saints, both the living and the righteous dead. However, Article XXII of the 39 Articles declares that the "Romish Doctrine concerning... Worshipping and Adoration, as well of Images as of Relics, and also Invocation of Saints, is a fond thing, vainly invented, and grounded upon no warranty of Scripture, but rather repugnant to the Word of God."

Episcopalians do commemorate the feast days (usually the date of death) of Christians whose lives and deeds have been exemplary, whether or not they were of major ecclesiastical significance. Such "saints" include Dr. Martin Luther King, Jr., William Wilberforce, and Elizabeth Cady Stanton. Liturgies for celebrating those feasts may be found in *Lesser Feasts and Fasts,* which contains material regarding various men and women the Church wishes to honor. In high-altitude Anglo-Catholic churches, prayers to the Virgin Mary and other saints are not unknown. There is no formal canonization process, such as the Roman Catholic Church has, but saints can be added to the Church's calendar by resolution of the General Convention, which meets every three years.

WHY EPISCOPALIANS DRESS UP (ESPECIALLY THE CLERGY)

When you meet the president you wear a tie.

When you go to your prom you rent a tux.

When you get married you break out the diamonds.

Let's face it, the most conspicuous way we show respect is with our wardrobe.

And that's the biggest reason many Episcopalians tend to dress for worship the way we do.

While it may come off as stubborn sentimentalism and mindless traditionalism (and, for some, it is), Episcopalians like to think that our Sunday morning worship commands an elevated sense of respect and honor. Sure, we're meeting one another, our close friends and family, but we are also meeting the Lord. And the Bible tells us that such occasions have, among other things, caused some people to remove their shoes, struck others blind, and even caused a donkey to talk (Numbers 22:28). So we may be getting off easy with a simple suit jacket.

Clergy usually lead the fashion parade. The bright colors, intricate patterns and high-quality fabrics worn by many of them are intended to impart a level of formality that is festive yet serious, celebrative yet sober. Clergy remind us of our core beliefs; that Christ is present in the Word proclaimed, in the gathered community (the Bible says, "wherever two or more are gathered in my name, I am present"), and in Holy Communion ("This is my body, this is my blood"). And if Christ is really present, then one way we recognize this is by dressing the way we do.

In our increasingly casual environment this is, admittedly, a hard sell.

We realize we're counter-cultural.

We know that lots of people might not see things this way.

Heck, not even all Episcopalians dress up for worship.

But that's OK. We know that no matter how people dress, Jesus shows up at millions of different churches on Sundays. Some of us just like to have our shoes polished when he comes.

DO EPISCOPALIANS LEAVE CHURCH EARLY?

It's not that we can't, it's just that we — don't.

Chalk it up to our proper English heritage, but few people seem to make a motion for the door until the last line of the last hymn is completed, and the deacon or priest gives the formal dismissal.

In fact, Episcopalians owe more than we're aware of to our deferential Anglican roots. As we know, all churches have a distinctive aesthetic, or DNA. Some of our proclivities are seen in

- the polite distance we tend to give visitors;

- our hesitancy to talk about money;

- our aversion to any kind of evangelism that would make someone feel uncomfortable;

- the particular gusto with which we sing our hymns;

- our desire to stick around until our worship services are officially over.

The formality of Episcopal worship is not intended to constrict; rather, it grows out of an understanding that boundaries aren't a bad thing — that games are actually better played when they have rules. Of course, that's not to say our rules are any better than anyone else's. But it is to say that we have them, and that the best way to learn them is by joining in. And you're invited to show up next Sunday for your first lesson.

IS COFFEE REALLY
THE THIRD SACRAMENT?

If we had one, this would certainly be in the running.

Following the main Sunday services at most Episcopal churches is a peculiar and rather friendly gathering with a highly creative name: Coffee Hour. As if the title doesn't give it away, this is an informal get-together of parish friends and family to catch up over a cup of coffee and warm conversation.

The importance of these gatherings cannot be under-estimated. Most Episcopal parishes are small (average attendance is 129 people on Sunday morning) and include generations of extended families. These people are godparents to each other's children, sponsors for confirmation, leaders on youth outings, etc. Given the depth of relationship, it is easy to understand why Coffee Hour is so important.

Of course this can make it difficult for a visitor to break in, and the best advice is patience. Or even better yet: introduce yourself. Like family reunions, Coffee Hour can take on an aura of excitement over familiar faces, and the newcomer can be unintentionally overlooked.

Coffee also plays an important part in the outreach ministries of many parishes. A lot of Episcopal churches host 12-step recovery programs whose life-blood tends to be coffee.

By the way, Episcopalians officially recognize only two sacraments, Baptism and Holy Communion, as those handed down by Jesus. Five more are highly regarded, and some Episcopalians also recognize them as sacraments: Confirmation, Marriage, Ordination, Confession (Reconciliation), and Holy Unction (Last Rites). No word on when Coffee Hour might be added.

WHAT TO BRING TO A CHURCH POTLUCK (BY REGION)

It is a generally followed practice in North American churches to enjoy three courses at potlucks (commonly referred to as "dishes"). Many of these dishes take on the flavor of the regions or cultures they represent. For best results, the preparer should understand the context in which the "dish" is presented.

The Salad

Potluck salads are quite different from actual salads. In preparation for making a potluck salad, ask yourself three questions:

- Is this dish mostly meat-free?
- Can this dish be served with a spoon or salad tongs?
- Can it be served chilled?

If the answer is "yes" to any of these questions, consider the dish a potluck-eligible salad.

The Mixture

This is the foundation of any potluck salad. It gives the salad a sense of direction. If at all possible, use ingredients that are indigenous to your area. For example, broccoli, lettuce, apples, macaroni, and candy bars are common in more temperate climates.

The Crunchy Stuff

This component gives life and pizzazz to an otherwise bland salad. Examples: tortilla chips, shoestring potato crisps, onion crisps, and fried pork rinds.

The Glue

The glue holds the salad together. The variety of available types is stunning, ranging from a traditional oil-based salad dressing to mayonnaise and non-dairy whipped topping. Use your imagination. Consult regional recipes for exact ingredients.

Note: Some salads are best when made well in advance and allowed to sit overnight. This is called *marinating,* or "controlled decomposition." Do not use actual glue adhesive. Other salads are best prepared immediately before serving.

The Casserole

A three-layered dish, typically. In order to make each casserole as culturally relevant as possible, use the following guidelines. Consult local restaurants for ideas, when in doubt.

Starch

East Coast: pasta or rice pilaf

Midwest: rice, potatoes, noodles, or more rice

South: grits

Southwest: black, red, or pinto beans

West Coast: tofu

Meat

East Coast: sausage or chicken

Midwest: ground beef—in a pinch, SPAM luncheon meat

South: crawdad or marlin

Southwest: pulled pork

West Coast: tofu

Cereal

East Coast: corn flakes

Midwest: corn flakes

South: corn flakes

Southwest: corn flakes

West Coast: tofu flakes

Note: The starch and meat may be mixed with a cream-based soup. The cereal must always be placed on the top of the casserole.

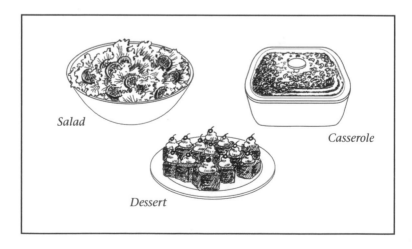

Salad

Casserole

Dessert

The Dessert

The most highly valued dish at a potluck, this can be the simplest and most fun to make. There are two key ingredients:

1. flour
2. fudge

Regional influences can be quite profound. The following are examples of typical desserts around the country. Consult your church's elders for the nuances of your region.

Cleveland: fudge brownies with fudge frosting

Kansas City: triple-fudge fudge with fudge sauce and a side of fudge

Los Angeles: tofu fudge

Miami: fudge

New York City: cheesecake with fudge drizzle

Be Aware

- Use caution when preparing a dish. Adding local ingredients to any meat, salad, or dessert can increase the fellowship factor of your potluck exponentially. It also raises the risk of a "flop."

- Always follow safe food-handling guidelines.

- Any combination of flavored gelatin, shredded carrots, mini-marshmallows, and canned pears is an acceptable "utility" dish, especially in the Midwest, should you be unable to prepare one from the above categories.

HOW TO JOIN
AN EPISCOPAL CHURCH

Just show up.

OK, this may not be the only requirement, but it is, by far, the most important.

Many Episcopal parishes are somewhat intentionally vague about assigning membership. We don't want to be known as places where weekly attendance is taken, annual contributions are tabulated, and your membership is assigned only if you pass muster. We are much less concerned about counting the people who are in, than we are about leaving someone out.

You can consult your local parish for details, but most follow a variation on what's specified by the Episcopal Church's Constitution and Canons, which govern all parishes and dioceses: baptism in this or any other Christian church, confirmation or reception by a bishop of the Episcopal Church or of a church in communion with the Episcopal Church (expected of all adult members), attendance, reception of Holy Communion, and some sort of financial commitment. Of course, some people claim membership to our churches because a long-lost relative once attended, and this is fine by us. We believe the church should reflect the open and accepting arms of Jesus.

If one is baptized in a parish, he or she automatically becomes a member. If one is already a member of an Episcopal parish and moves to another, a Letter of Transfer is typically requested. However, the paperwork generally plays second fiddle to the importance of a particular faith community in one's life: is this particular church "home"? If so (and we hope it is), you're in.

And, keep showing up!

HOW TO GET MARRIED
IN AN EPISCOPAL CHURCH

They're a Hollywood location scout's dream.

Many Episcopal parishes make idyllic backdrops for couples making some of the most important promises of their lives. The traditional architecture, the highly polished brass, and timeworn pews all contribute to the high demand for weddings that some parishes experience. And most are very happy to accommodate starry-eyed couples.

Of course, marriage is not built on buildings. It's built on people who make commitments. And the Episcopal Church wants to make sure that every marriage has the very best chance of succeeding. The Church requires that at least the bride or groom be a baptized Christian. If neither is, we'll work toward this before the wedding date. We also need some time before the wedding for proper pre-marital counseling. There are also county and state requirements that need to be satisfied in order for weddings to happen.

Episcopalians love weddings. We see them as an earthly representation of the mysterious union between Christ and Christ's Church. The love of two people that leads them toward life-long commitment to one another reflects God's commitment to always be by our side. And since God accepts all of us, some of our parishes also offer the blessing of same-gender couples. So the bottom line is, if you'd like to get married in an Episcopal Church, contact the parish you're interested in and ask about their particular guidelines. They differ slightly from place to place, but each is intended to help the marriage succeed, flourish, and outlast any church building.

HOW TO GET RE-MARRIED IN AN EPISCOPAL CHURCH

For a church whose heritage includes the oft-married King Henry VIII, you'd think we'd be good at this one. But the fact is, divorce is rarely good; it is difficult, painful, and sometimes, the best option available.

The Episcopal Church sees marriage as a human endeavor, almost always entered into with the best of intentions. But, like everything else we attempt, we can fail no matter how hard we try. This is why annulments and the renunciation of a previous relationship are generally not required in the Episcopal Church. When marriages fail, we believe the best place to go to put our lives back together is the church. Divorced people are welcome at our churches and at our Communion rail. The counsel of clergy and the friendship of parishioners have helped countless people through this agonizing experience.

However, once a divorce has occurred and remarriage becomes a possibility, there are a few considerations to keep in mind. These have to do with taking care of the responsibilities arising out of the previous relationship; i.e., children, property, etc. The overriding concerns have to do with responsibility, honesty, and integrity. Divorce and remarriage are intimate affairs and best left to the counsel of your local Episcopal clergyperson, who would be happy to answer any questions.

HOW TO ENROLL YOUR CHILD IN SUNDAY SCHOOL

Just as Jesus beckoned children to come to him (Matthew 19:13), so does his church.

Like most churches, the Episcopal Church offers a wide variety of children's Sunday School and Christian educational programming. Some of the more popular (and worth Googling) are the Catechesis of the Good Shepherd, Godly Play, Worship Center, and Journey to Adulthood. The Episcopal Church requires all Sunday school teachers to go through background checks and special training before they are allowed to teach children. Children are God's gift to parents and to churches and we do the best we can to safeguard our young ones.

Because Episcopal parishes tend to be small, class sizes are small too, which provides a better student–teacher ratio. Classes are offered at most parishes throughout the program year (September-May) and may include Vacation Bible School, summer mission trips, and pilgrimages.

Since the Episcopal Church does not believe that children are the "future" of the church — they *are* the church — we welcome their participation in various leadership capacities. Once a youngster turns 16, he or she is welcome to serve on the vestry (aka church board). They are also encouraged to take leadership roles in various diocesan, provincial, and national church activities.

If you are interested in finding out what's offered at your local Episcopal parish, give them a call. If you want to find a parish close to you, go to *www.theredbook.org.*

HOW TO BECOME A CHRISTIAN

To most Episcopalians, this is a puzzling question.

That's because many of us were baptized as children and raised in Christian homes. Many of us have never not known what it is like to be a Christian. This is a common tendency among Christians in liturgical churches like ours.

On the other end of the spectrum we find faith communities that constantly ask and explain what it is to "come to Jesus." This is particularly appealing to people who have either never been exposed to Christianity, or who never quite understood what their own church stood for. That's why it is particularly important for those of us in liturgical churches to remind ourselves of what it is that makes us who we are.

Becoming a Christian is, and is not, difficult. The easy part is renouncing our sins, turning to Christ as savior, and pledging to repent when we sin. The hard part is actually doing it. Episcopalians use the words of our Baptismal Covenant (BCP, page 304, and page 228 of this book). Not only is this recited at our baptism, but at all baptisms (several times a year). We recognize the importance of reminding ourselves of our pledge to follow Christ. We nurture it by coming to church regularly, partaking of Holy Communion, and praying frequently.

If you are interested in becoming a Christian, read up on the Baptismal Covenant, talk to an Episcopalian, or contact your local Episcopal clergyperson.

WHAT TO SAY AT A FUNERAL

Episcopalians are not a demonstrative people, by and large, and so funerals in the Episcopal tradition are generally quite low-key. The focus of the service is on the promise of the Resurrection, but rarely are the bereaved quite ready to hear that from anyone save the clergy. Simplicity and judicious honesty is best.

Do say:

I am so sorry for your loss.
[Name of deceased] was a good person. S/he will be missed.
Would you like a hug?
I have never been through something like this and can only imagine what you feel, but please know that I am praying for you.
What do you need right now?
I am here to listen whenever you are ready.
Please accept my deepest sympathy to you and your family.

Under no circumstances should you essay the following responses. They are grounds for justifiable and immediate homicide:

Only the good die young.
God must have needed another angel/needed him more than we do.
You'll find someone else (or, you'll have other children).
Don't worry. You'll see him/her again.
At least s/he didn't suffer long.
S/he is in a better place.
Be thankful s/he doesn't have to experience pain and heartache on this earth any more.
Doesn't s/he look natural?*

*Inevitably someone will think of the Bill Cosby comedy routine of many years ago, risking inappropriate laughter.

WHY MORE PEOPLE DON'T GO TO CHURCH

Actually, a fair number of Americans do. The Gallup Organization has been measuring church attendance since World War II and finds that Americans, year after year, self-report a 40 percent church-going rate on any given Sunday. Due to flaws in self-reporting (Americans typically say they vote more than they do and say they visit porn sites much less than they do), this number is probably much smaller, perhaps 25 to 30 percent, which is still a sizable number.

However, some 85 percent of Americans identify themselves as Christians. Most Americans say they believe in God and are spiritual people. So what keeps people from joining a church? Like bowling leagues, women's social groups, and political parties, people just aren't joining civic organizations like they used to. Things have drastically changed since the 1950s, which was a high-water mark for church attendance. We are no longer a "joining" culture. Sure, there are the economic and social forces that propelled women into the workplace and have us all working more. But perhaps more telling is an increase in highly individualistic activities like television watching and surfing the fathomless Internet.

However, this is not to say that churches are blameless. Churches are not unlike restaurants: people will stand in line when they find a good one. It is incumbent upon us to do the kinds of things and be the kind of people that has made Christianity such an important part of our lives. Americans are hungry for meaning, purpose, and adventure. These are all integral to living the Christian life. The Church has myriad amazing possibilities before it: to help end hunger, combat racism, end war, and stand up for human rights (just to name a few). The churches that are most deeply involved in changing the world may be best equipped to get people to church on Sundays.

WHY (MOST) EPISCOPALIANS DON'T KICK DOGS

We don't advocate hitting kittens or starting forest fires, either.

In fact, caring for all of God's creation is something Episcopalians have long been interested in doing. Our Baptismal Covenant (see page 228) calls us to strive for justice and peace, which includes everything that God has created.

This is why many Episcopal congregations sponsor an annual "Blessing of the Animals." It's often held in the fall, around the feast day of St. Francis of Assisi (October 4). Some churches, like the Cathedral of St. John the Divine in New York, have welcomed horses, elephants, and camels into their sanctuary. Most others stick with dogs and cats, though iguanas, gerbils, and even snakes get in line. (Note to service planners: keep the gerbils and snakes at opposite ends of the church.) The Episcopal Network for Animal Welfare (*www.franciscan-anglican.com/enaw*), a sister organization to the Anglican Society for the Welfare of Animals, works to raise awareness of issues of animal cruelty and abuse.

Another grassroots organization working toward better stewardship of God's creation is the Episcopal Ecological Network (*www.eenonline.org*). This group advocates for the protection of the environment and preserving the sanctity of creation. When the heavens and the earth were created, God called it good — and we believe it still is. This is why we seek to not only care for it, as God has, but to bless it, as God continues to do.

WHY 70% OF EPISCOPALIANS WEREN'T BORN THAT WAY

Yes, we're a church of refugees.

It's no secret that the clear majority of those in Episcopal Church pews on Sunday mornings were not born Episcopalians. Most of us came from other Christian denominations or from no church background at all. So, what's the draw?

Since many converts come as adults, chances are logic and reason play a role in a person's decision to become an Episcopalian. The Episcopal Church has consistently been labeled a "middle road" — a *"via media"* — between Roman Catholicism and Protestantism. We bring the reverence and rootedness of an ancient tradition alongside a clear devotion to the Bible and priesthood of all believers. In years past, in fact, some people suggested that were America to unite under one, central religion, it just might be the Episcopal Church. It's worth noting that the National Cathedral in Washington, DC, host to some of the nation's most important religious events, is an Episcopal church.

Other people become Episcopalians because of our views on Holy Communion, women's ordination, and human rights. Some love the music. Others marry into the church. And some come because it's convenient (there are some 7,200 Episcopal Church congregations in the United States, Europe, Haiti, and Central America). No matter why people come, we like to think that we are a place of welcome. Wherever people are on their spiritual journey, our parishes strive to receive them with joy, understanding, and warmth. We don't pressure people or force them to believe one thing or another. Rather, our congregations tend to thrive by providing an atmosphere of open curiosity, allowing people to ask and answer their own questions. We strive to let the Holy Spirit work. And when we do this, we find many people choosing the Episcopal Church.

WHY THE EPISCOPAL CHURCH IS (AND ISN'T) CATHOLIC LITE

It's both a catchy joke and an apt description — Catholic Lite.

Comedian Robin Williams (an Episcopalian) popularized this term in an interview when, referring to a beer commercial, he described Catholic Lite as "same rituals, half the guilt." Like all jokes, there's a nugget of truth in there, and one we're rather proud of.

The Episcopal Church is a proud descendant of the Church of England, which was rooted in the Roman Catholic Church. A variety of factors led to this split some 500 years ago, and it's one that we're still working to heal. But we are indebted and appreciative of the many rituals, traditions, and ways of believing in Christ that have come to us through our Catholic roots.

And like the Roman Catholic Church, the Episcopal Church has changed and evolved. We have come down on the same side of most issues, and on different sides of others. We are perceived as being less strict, allowing priests to marry and non-Episcopalians to take Holy Communion, and publicly allowing a wider breadth of acceptable belief and practice than one might find in a Roman Catholic Church.

However, the idea that being an Episcopalian lacks rigor and demand is the down side to Williams' description. There is nothing "lite" about being a Christian, no matter what denomination one might choose. Episcopalians promise in their baptisms to pray, take communion, and to spread the Gospel just like most other Christians.

DO EPISCOPALIANS BELIEVE IN CONFIRMATION?

Sure.

However, like many Christians, we have our own take on it. Episcopalians believe confirmation is an important step in the spiritual development of all believers, especially those baptized at an early age. In this case, it is expected that when one is ready and has been prepared, a public affirmation of faith be made. This is a pledge to recommit to the responsibilities in the Baptismal Covenant (see page 228).

Some parishes recommend a particular age, say 13 or 14, while others wait until a young person expresses interest. While confirmation used to be tied to the acceptance of Holy Communion, this is no longer the case as all are welcome to receive Holy Communion following baptism.

Confirmation also includes the laying on of hands by a bishop. When the bishop does this, the bishop also prays that the Holy Spirit would come upon the candidate. Bishops are our earthly representatives of those first disciples; that's why they wear that pointy hat called a mitre. It's supposed to look like a tongue of fire, symbolic of the tongues of fire that descended upon the first disciples on a holy day called Pentecost, and symbolic of what's happening when one is confirmed.

So confirmation is all about gearing up and energizing the spiritual life of a young person — or any person. This is why Episcopalians make available a similar rite called "Reaffirmation of Baptismal Vows" to all confirmed Christians. This is aimed at helping us reinvigorate our spiritual lives at any age.

DO EPISCOPALIANS BELIEVE IN THE CREEDS?

Believe in them? We even memorize them!

Like most churches, Episcopalians have a high regard for the historic creeds of the Christian faith. You will find the Nicene Creed included in the main Sunday services at nearly every Episcopal church. The Apostles' Creed is found in the daily prayers suggested in the Book of Common Prayer, and is recited at baptismal services.

These creeds are more than 1,500 years old and are widely regarded as embodying the essentials of the Christian faith. They describe our understanding of God the Father, Son, and Holy Spirit, as well as the place and role of the church. When we recite them on Sundays we realize we are not only confirming our unity with millions of other Christians around the world, but with even millions more who have preceded us in the faith.

Also included in the Book of Common Prayer is the Creed of Saint Athanasius, which is found toward the back in a section labeled "Historical Documents." This is not normally recited at worship, but is included as a reference alongside other writings that have shaped the Episcopal Church.

The creeds play an important role in the ongoing formation of the Episcopal Church. We continue to rely on their principles as we take our faith into the new millennium.

DO EPISCOPALIANS GO TO CONFESSION?

All may, some should, and none must.

This is a popular way of describing what many Episcopalians believe about Confession, or, as it's more correctly labeled, Reconciliation of the Penitent.

Yes, Episcopalians believe in this rite. We have a liturgy for it in the Book of Common Prayer (page 447). It is open and recommended to all Episcopalians, though few seem to take advantage of it. Maybe it's because many of us don't see the need to get a priest involved and take 1 John 1:9 literally: "If we confess our sins, he who is faithful and just will forgive us our sins and cleanse us from all unrighteousness."

However, when people do take advantage of this rite it is often in the spring, during Holy Week. A priest commonly serves as the confessor, as priests and bishops are the only ones permitted to grant absolution. Episcopalians also believe any Christian can hear a confession and grant a simple Declaration of Forgiveness.

This rite is typically carried out in privacy and in a worship area, with the confessor sitting behind the altar rail and the penitent kneeling, although face-to-face reconciliation in church pews or in a clergyperson's office is increasingly popular. After the confession is heard the confessor may give counsel and encouragement, and even assign a psalm, prayer, or something to be done as a sign of penitence and thanksgiving.

The contents of all confessions are not normally a matter of subsequent conversation. And when made to a priest or bishop, confidentiality is morally absolute for the confessor and may not, under any circumstances, be broken.

HOW EPISCOPALIANS USE THREE-LEGGED STOOLS

Just like dairy farmers.

Of course, Episcopalians use three-legged stools to sit firmly and securely while we go about our work. However, we also use the three-legged stool as a metaphor for the way we define authority in the Episcopal Church.

The three legs are the Bible, tradition, and reason, in this order. Holy Scripture is paramount as a way of defining what we believe and how we believe it. Does that mean we take the Bible literally? Not usually, though we do take it seriously (more on page 150).

When Episcopalians talk about tradition, we are referring to the many ways that the saints before us have dealt with issues of faith and doctrine. Let's face it, there are many modern concerns upon which the Bible is more or less silent, like nuclear warfare and premarital sex, so we consult the thoughts and writings of pious ancestors in the tradition to help us make a way forward.

The third leg is reason. By this we mean the very broadest horizon of human understanding, along with the deepest well of personal experience. Of course, reason is far from perfect; we know we always run the risk of falling into rationalism. But we also realize that one of God's greatest gifts is that part of the human body that rests between our shoulders.

Thus, when it comes to defining faith and doctrine, unless we have all three legs grounded and balanced, the whole enterprise topples over. This means that whether we are talking about matters of religion, or milking a cow, keeping a modicum of stability is of great importance.

WHY ARE EPISCOPALIANS SO WISHY-WASHY?

Talk about the bland leading the bland...

For centuries Episcopalians have had this nagging milquetoast reputation. We're not comfortable being in the spotlight, we're often willing to listen to both sides of an argument, and compromise sits well with the vast majority of us. Some people criticize us for being unwilling to take a stand. Others compliment us for our even-handedness. So why do Episcopalians luxuriate in the lackluster?

The penchant we have for compromise comes to us quite naturally. As spiritual progeny of the Church of England, Episcopalians have inherited an English proclivity toward finding middle ground between two extremes. It's called the *via media*. Formed amidst the battles between Catholics and Protestants in the fifteenth century, the Church of England embraced and promoted compromise as a way to stop the quarreling (and killing) and get on with the work of proclaiming the Gospel of Jesus Christ.

On a practical level we all know that the truth rarely lies in the extreme, but somewhere in the middle. That's why most Episcopal churches are known for their openness and willingness to listen. Years ago we promoted ourselves as a place where "you don't need to check your brains at the door," where open and honest dialogue is welcomed. This sense of balance may be one reason for this fact: more U.S. Supreme Court justices have been Episcopalians than any other religion.

A SHORT CHRONOLOGY OF THE EPISCOPAL CHURCH

1607   Founding of Jamestown colony in Virginia. Robert Hunt, priest, celebrates Holy Eucharist and leads daily Morning and Evening Prayer.

1624   Virginia becomes a royal colony, required to conform to Church of England (though without a bishop, confirmations, ordinations, etc.).

1701   Thomas Bray, priest, put in charge of church work in Maryland, founds Society for the Propagation of the Gospel, which sponsors over 300 missionaries in the colonies over the next century.

1738   John and Charles Wesley and George Whitefield, all Anglican priests, have religious experiences in Georgia. Evangelicalism gains popularity.

1776   Declaration of Independence by American colonies. Two-thirds of the signers are nominal members of the Church of England, but they do not want the colonies to be governed by bishops. Many Anglicans flee to Canada or remain as Tories.

1779   Charles Simeon, a scrupulous college student, becomes a priest and noted Anglican evangelical leader.

1784   Samuel Seabury consecrated first American bishop by Scottish bishops.

1789   First General Convention of the Episcopal Church, held in Philadelphia. House of Bishops and House of Deputies established. The Book of Common Prayer is revised and adopted.

1794 St. Thomas' African Episcopal Church admitted to the Diocese of Pennsylvania.

1804 Absalom Jones, the Episcopal Church's first black priest, ordained.

1833 John Keble, Edward Pusey, and John Henry Newman founded the Oxford Movement.

1835 Jackson Kemper ordained bishop and is first missionary bishop to American frontier.

1871 Order of deaconesses revived.

1888 Chicago-Lambeth Quadrilateral on church unity adopted. William Reed Huntington, priest, is author.

1889 United Thank Offering is founded.

1948 World Council of Churches convenes in Amsterdam as a "fellowship of churches which confess Jesus Christ as God and Savior." Archbishop of Canterbury Geoffrey Fisher presides.

1974 Eleven women ordained as priests in Philadelphia, Pennsylvania.

1976 Episcopal Church General Convention approves ordination of women to all three orders: bishop, priest, and deacon.

1989 Barbara Harris consecrated bishop suffragan of Massachusetts: first woman bishop in the Anglican Communion.

2003 Gene Robinson, an openly gay priest, consecrated as bishop of New Hampshire.

2006 Katharine Jefferts Schori elected and consecrated first female Presiding Bishop of the Episcopal Church and first female primate in the Anglican Communion.

FIVE EPISCOPALIANS
WHO SHAPED THE CHURCH

1 **Samuel Seabury**

He was our first bishop. Part of the reason the Episcopal Church formed was because the Church of England refused to post a bishop in the American colonies, necessitating a long, arduous journey back to England every time someone needed to be confirmed or ordained as a priest. Following the Revolutionary War, Seabury, who hailed from Connecticut, traveled to England in 1783. Since he could no longer take an oath of allegiance to the king, Seabury went to Scotland to be consecrated. He returned to America and he put his superior organizational and liturgical gifts to work, laying a firm foundation for the Episcopal Church.

2 **William White**

Since it takes three bishops to consecrate a bishop, no sooner had Samuel Seabury returned from Scotland than the young American church put forward another candidate for bishop, William White of Philadelphia. By the time he arrived in England in 1787, the atmosphere had become more welcoming toward Americans, so he, along with Samuel Provoost of New York, were consecrated as our second and third bishops. White was a devout pastor, founding several charitable and educational institutions to help the poor, the deaf, and the very first home devoted to helping prostitutes. White also served as the Episcopal Church's first Presiding Bishop.

❸ John Henry Hobart

Arguably one of the most ambitious and hard-working clergyman our church has ever seen, Hobart was utterly devoted to the work of the Episcopal Church. Ordained bishop in New York in 1811 at the young age of 36, Hobart traveled 2,000 miles each winter for visitations and twice that distance in the summer. During 19 years as bishop, his diocese grew from 50 parishes to nearly 170, and the number of clergy increased from 26 to 133. Hobart founded the General Theological Seminary in New York City and Geneva College in upstate New York (now called Hobart College). In his later years Hobart was so popular many considered him a viable candidate for governor.

❹ Philips Brooks

Widely regarded as the best preacher of the nineteenth century, Brooks was an outspoken critic of slavery. Graduating from Harvard at age 20, he went on to Virginia Theological Seminary and served parishes in Philadelphia and Boston. He preached noteworthy sermons to large crowds, many of which are still read today. He is probably best known as the author of the Christmas carol, "O Little Town of Bethlehem." Brooks was elected the sixth bishop of Massachusetts and served for just 15 months before his death, which was a major event in Boston's history.

❺ Barbara Harris

She is the first woman to be consecrated bishop not only in the Episcopal Church, but also in the Anglican Communion. Harris, the former head of public relations for the Sun Oil Company, was long interested in civil rights. She participated in freedom rides and marches in the South in the 1960s. After discerning a call to ministry, she was ordained priest in 1980. She served as publisher and later board member of the Episcopal Church Publishing Company's progressive magazine, *The Witness*. She was consecrated as a bishop suffragan (aka "assistant") in 1989 in the Diocese of Massachusetts, where she served for 13 years until her retirement.

FIVE INSPIRING BLACK EPISCOPALIANS

1 Absalom Jones

Born a slave in Delaware in 1746, Absalom Jones went on to become what many believe was the first black American to receive formal ordination in any denomination. A contemporary of Richard Allen, founder of the African Methodist Episcopal Church (AME Zion), Jones was also a well-known Philadelphia abolitionist and orator, preaching often (and memorably) against slavery. Jones petitioned Congress regarding the 1793 Fugitive Slave Act, lobbying for leniency and better treatment for blacks. He was the founder of the African Episcopal Church of St. Thomas, which continues as a vibrant congregation. The Episcopal Church honors his life each February 13.

2 Thurgood Marshall

He has been called the most important African-American of the twentieth century. Marshall was the first African-American to serve on the United States Supreme Court. He crisscrossed the South, filing civil rights lawsuits on behalf of the NAACP. He argued and won 29 of 32 cases before the Supreme Court. Marshall may be best remembered for winning the 1954 *Brown vs. Board of Education* case, which declared segregation in public schools unconstitutional. Marshall worshiped at St. Augustine's in southwest Washington, DC, where a community center there bears his name.

❸ John Burgess

John Burgess served as bishop in the Episcopal Diocese of Massachusetts for 13 years, first as bishop suffragan from 1962 to 1969. He was elected as bishop coadjutor in 1969 and served as diocesan bishop from 1970 to 1975 — thus becoming the first African-American to head a diocese in the Episcopal Church. While serving as Episcopal chaplain at historically black Howard University in Washington, DC, Burgess was also named a canon at Washington National Cathedral. His preaching there in the 1950s roused the social conscience of the Episcopal Church and nurtured the seeds of the church's involvement in the civil rights movement. Burgess was known for his commitment to the welfare of the urban poor and for his desire that the Church be a force for social change beyond its doors. "I just wanted to prove that the Episcopal Church could be relevant to the lives of the poor," he said in a 1992 interview.

❹ Colin Powell

The son of Jamaican immigrants, General Colin Luther Powell was raised in New York's South Bronx, where he served as an acolyte at St. Margaret's Episcopal Church. He calls the Episcopal Church a pillar of his life, and says it helped instill the discipline, structure, camaraderie, and the sense of belonging that became very important to him as his career took off. At age 49, he became President Ronald Reagan's National Security Advisor. At 52, he became the youngest person — and first African-American — to serve as Chairman of the Joint Chiefs of Staff. In 2001, under President George W. Bush, he became the first African-American U.S. Secretary of State.

❺ James Holly

Born to freed slaves in Washington, DC, James Theodore Holly became the first African-American bishop of the Episcopal Church as well as the first bishop of Haiti. Ordained at age 27, Holly served as rector of St. Luke's Church in New Haven, Connecticut, where in 1856 he founded the Protestant Episcopal Society for Promoting the Extension of the Church Among Colored People, which eventually became the Union of Black Episcopalians (*www.ube.org*), lobbying for the inclusion of blacks in Episcopal seminaries and diocesan conventions. In 1861 he left for Haiti, where he organized churches, schools and medical facilities. He was later given charge of the Episcopal Church in the Dominican Republic. The Episcopal Church honors his life every March 13.

FIVE INSPIRING
FEMALE EPISCOPALIANS

① Amelia Bloomer

Here was a passionate supporter of women's rights who lent her name to those frilly pants called "bloomers." Originally from upstate New York, she wrote passionately about important women's issues such as equal education, temperance, suffrage and fashion. In 1850, she began wearing a style of loose-fitting pants in response to tight-fitting corsets that sometimes caused health problems and physical deformities. She joined the Episcopal Church in her twenties. The Church honors her feast day on July 20 along with fellow women's right supporters Harriet Tubman, Elizabeth Cady Stanton, and Sojourner Truth.

② Eleanor Roosevelt

One of the most admired women of the twentieth century, Anna Eleanor Roosevelt was First Lady of the United States from 1933–1945. Known as a reformer, diplomat, and humanitarian, she was a cradle Episcopalian, making her church home at St. James' in Hyde Park, New York. Along with raising five children and supporting her husband, Franklin Delano Roosevelt, she was an outspoken advocate of equal rights, child welfare, and labor reforms. She served as the U.S. delegate to the United Nations and played a key role in the adoption of the Universal Declaration of Human Rights in 1948.

❸ Katharine Jefferts Schori

She is the first woman Presiding Bishop of the Episcopal Church and the first female primate in the entire Anglican Communion. Enthroned in 2006, her leadership has emphasized advocacy for the poor and marginalized. She is a strong proponent of the United Nations' Millennium Development Goals and an outspoken advocate on environmental issues. During her time in office, Jefferts Schori has been challenged in keeping both conservative and liberal elements of the church together. She has a background in biology and oceanography, and is a licensed pilot. As bishop of Nevada, she piloted her plane around the diocese for visitations.

❹ Sandra Day O'Connor

This esteemed jurist was the first woman to serve on the United States Supreme Court. Appointed by President Ronald Reagan in 1981, Justice O'Connor served the high court for 24 years before retiring. During this time she was consistently voted one of America's most powerful women. A cradle Episcopalian, her gender made her unable to work as an attorney following graduation from Stanford University law school. So she turned to public service in California, then Germany, then in her home state of Arizona. She was elected judge in Maricopa County in 1975. Her professionalism and fairness made her one of the most respected judges in recent memory.

❺ Pamela Pauly Chinnis

Pamela Chinnis is the first woman to serve as President of the Episcopal Church's House of Deputies. She was elected in 1991, 1994, and 1997 for three three-year terms. Her presidency, coming only 21 years after the first woman deputy was granted seat, voice, and vote in the House of Deputies, marked a major milestone in the leadership of lay women in the highest levels of Episcopal Church governance. She was a staunch supporter of the role of the House of Deputies, repeatedly reminding its members that it was the "senior" house and that "the House of Deputies was a complete innovation when this church was organized following the American Revolution. Laity, clergy and bishops have an equal voice in determining policy, establishing our legal framework and maintaining a living liturgical life." A resident of Washington, DC, she worshiped and served in numerous leadership roles at Church of the Epiphany and served on the cathedral chapter of Washington National Cathedral.

FIVE FAMOUS EPISCOPALIAN WRITERS

❶ John Steinbeck

Instantly recognized by many a high school literature student, John Steinbeck is probably best known for his works of Depression-era fiction, *The Grapes of Wrath* (1939) and *Of Mice and Men* (1937). Steinbeck won the Pulitzer Prize and the Nobel Prize for literature. He published a total of 25 books (which, in turn, led to the sales of countless copies of Cliff Notes...). Steinbeck was born and raised in Salinas, California. He served as an acolyte and choir member at St. Paul's Episcopal Church in Salinas where, it is said, he dropped a cross onto a visiting bishop's head and thus lost his head acolyte privileges. Many of Steinbeck's books were also made into plays and films, including *Tortilla Flat* (1942), *The Red Pony* (1949), and *East of Eden* (1955).

❷ Madeline L'Engle

A prolific writer of young adult fiction, L'Engle is probably best known for her Newbery Medal-winning novel, *A Wrinkle in Time* (1962) and its sequels, *A Wind in the Door* (1973), *A Swiftly Tilting Planet* (1978), *Many Waters* (1986) and *An Acceptable Time* (1989). L'Engle's writings exhibit a strong interest in modern science as well as religion. She became a volunteer librarian at the Cathedral of St. John the Divine in New York City in 1965. Years later she was named writer-in-residence there. L'Engle's controversial belief in universal salvation informed her stories. She was criticized by some Christians as liberal and at the same time by secular critics for being too religious.

3 **William Faulkner**

One of the most influential authors of the twentieth century, Faulkner was a prolific writer of novels and short stories. He won two Pulitzer Prizes and the Nobel Prize. His most popular works include *The Sound and the Fury* (1929), *As I Lay Dying* (1930), *Light in August* (1932), *Absalom, Absalom!* (1936), and "A Rose for Emily" (1932). Most of his stories were based in his native Mississippi, where he attended services at St. Peter's Episcopal Church in Oxford. Faulkner was known for his "Southern Gothic" stream of consciousness writing. Though not an outwardly religious man, his gifts of creativity and intelligence earned him an unparalleled place in American literary history.

4 **Harriet Beecher Stowe**

This famous American author and abolitionist is best known as the writer of *Uncle Tom's Cabin* (1852). The book brought home the horrors of slavery to millions of people. The daughter of famed Congregational minister Lyman Beecher, Harriet attended Episcopal services in Florida in the 1870s and 1880s. Her husband started a Bible study group which grew to become the Church of Our Saviour in Mandarin, Florida. Stowe wrote 30 books and countless shorter pieces. Many historians believe the publication of *Uncle Tom's Cabin* was a significant force leading up to the Civil War. Upon meeting Stowe, Abraham Lincoln allegedly declared, "So you're the little woman that started this great war!"

❺ Tennessee Williams

A legendary American playwright whose works won numerous awards, Thomas Lanier "Tennessee" Williams was the grandson of an Episcopal priest with whom he was particularly close. After suffering from a paralytic disease as a young boy, his mother gave him a typewriter. Williams would go on to write *The Glass Menagerie* (1945), *A Streetcar Named Desire* (1948), *The Rose Tattoo* (1952), and *Cat on a Hot Tin Roof* (1965). Later in life he attended Roman Catholic services. His literary rights now belong to Sewanee, The University of the South, an Episcopal school, which uses the funds to support a creative writing program.

FIVE FAMOUS EPISCOPALIAN PERFORMERS (OK, TEN)

❶ Robin Williams

One of the most popular comedians of the twentieth century, Williams has won numerous awards, including an Oscar, six Golden Globes, and a Screen Actors Guild award. His film credits include *Good Morning Vietnam* (1987), *Dead Poets Society* (1989), *Mrs. Doubtfire* (1993), and *Good Will Hunting* (1997). He is known for his extraordinary improvisational skills and spot-on impersonations. Not long ago, Williams was voted thirteenth on *Comedy Central Presents: 100 Greatest Stand-Ups of All Time*. Raised in a parish in suburban Detroit, Williams has never been timid about making fun of his WASP roots. "I'm an Episcopalian," he once said, "It's Catholic Lite — same rituals, half the guilt." Williams also came up with the oft-quoted "Top Ten Reasons to Be An Episcopalian."

❷ Judy Garland

One of Hollywood's most acclaimed entertainers, Judy Garland's versatility garnered her many awards, though she lived a difficult life. She won an Academy Award, a Golden Globe, Grammy awards, and a Tony. She is perhaps best known as Dorothy from *The Wizard of Oz* (1939) and her memorable rendition of "Somewhere Over the Rainbow." Born Frances Ethel Gumm in Grand Rapids, Minnesota, she was baptized at the local Episcopal parish where her father, a vaudeville performer, served as choral director. Garland starred in dozens of productions, including *Meet Me in St. Louis* (1944), *Easter Parade* (1948), and *A Star is Born* (1954). Married five times, Garland endured a decades-long struggle with addiction before her death at age 47. Her legacy includes daughter Liza Minnelli and a ranking among the American Film Institute's top ten greatest female stars in the history of American cinema.

❸ Courtney Cox Arquette

She's probably best known as one of the lead characters in the popular long running sitcom, *Friends*. Courtney Cox Arquette began her public career as a model, then appeared in a Bruce Springsteen video ("Dancing in the Dark"), and a few supporting television roles before landing a lead role in the ensemble cast of *Friends*. She married actor David Arquette at Grace Cathedral in San Francisco during her ten-year run on the sitcom. A few years later they returned to Cox Arquette's hometown of Birmingham, Alabama, where their first child, Coco Riley, was baptized at St. Stephen's Episcopal Church. Actress Jennifer Aniston is the child's godmother.

❹ Bono

Born Paul David Hewson, Bono is not an Episcopalian but his affiliation with the (Anglican) Church of Ireland and his inspiration for the popular U2Charist movement make him an honorary member. As lead singer and chief lyricist of the wildly popular band U2, Bono often uses social and religious themes in his songs. He is the only person to have been nominated for an Academy Award, Golden Globe, Grammy, and Nobel Peace Prize (for his work to end world poverty). U2 has won 22 Grammy Awards. Their hits include "Sunday, Bloody Sunday" (1983), "I Still Haven't Found What I'm Looking For" (1987), and "Beautiful Day" (2000). Bono was raised attending both Roman Catholic and Church of Ireland services. He was married in a Church of Ireland service and the family is known to attend a Church of Ireland parish. U2 inspired the popular U2Charist celebrations, which uses the band's repertoire as a backdrop for a socially conscious Episcopal worship service.

❺ Rosanne Cash

Often classified as a country musician, largely because of the success of her father, Johnny Cash, Rosanne Cash's music includes pop, rock, and folk influences. Cash joined her father's traveling show when she graduated from high school and gradually worked her way up to singing back-up vocals. After finally going out on her own, she had several country hits including "Seven Year Ache" (1981), "It's Such a Small World" (with Rodney Crowell, 1988), and "Runaway Train" (1988). Although her mother was a strict Roman Catholic and her father was a Baptist, Cash felt they were open to allowing her to undertake her own spiritual journey, which includes attending Episcopal services. "I consider myself religious in the best sense of the word . . . I pray every single day and I meditate every single day. So my spiritual life is as important to me as my creative life."

❻ Sam Waterston

An Academy Award-nominated actor, Sam Waterston is probably best known for his role on the long-running television series *Law and Order*. Waterston began playing the role of D.A. Jack McCoy in 1994. Nominated for a Best Actor Academy Award in 1985 for *The Killing Fields*, Waterston has won a Primetime Emmy, a Golden Globe, and a Screen Actors Guild award. A classically trained theater actor, other credits include *The Great Gatsby* (1974), *Crimes and Misdemeanors* (1989), and many award-winning performances in numerous Shakespeare productions. An active humanitarian and Episcopalian, Waterston has aided Refugees International, Meals on Wheels, the United Way, and the Episcopal Actors' Guild, and has chaired fundraising activities for the General Theological Seminary in New York City.

❼ Fred Astaire

Many believe him to be the most talented dancer of the twentieth century. Fred Astaire was an Oscar-winning film star and Broadway stage dancer, choreographer, singer, and actor. He paired with Ginger Rogers in ten films, including *Top Hat* (1935), *Swing Time* (1936), and *Shall We Dance* (1937). He was a talented though modest singer who also co-wrote (with Johnny Mercer) the top-ten hit, "I'm Building Up to an Awful Letdown" (1936). While not yet a teenager, the young Astaire met an Episcopal priest in New York City and was confirmed at the Church of the Transfiguration, which became home to the Episcopal Actors' Guild. During his life he is said to have enjoyed the quiet and calming atmosphere of St. Bartholomew's in New York City as well as All Saints' in Beverly Hills, California, where he spent long hours of contemplation.

❽ Judy Collins

Known for her distinctive soprano voice and her wide repertoire, Grammy winner Judy Collins came of age during the 1960s folk revival, singing songs by Bob Dylan and Pete Seeger. Her piercing eyes were the inspiration for Crosby, Stills, and Nash's hit song, "Suite: Judy Blue Eyes." Her versions of "Amazing Grace" and "Send in the Clowns" were top 20 hits. Collins' version of Joni Mitchell's "Chelsea Morning" inspired Bill and Hillary Clinton in naming their daughter. Raised in the

United Methodist Church, Collins married husband Louis Nelson at the Cathedral of St. John the Divine in New York City, where to this day she often goes to pray. "I think of Jesus as a total rebel because he was saying things that were completely out — forgive your enemies? Are you kidding? What a concept. Very revolutionary, actually."

9 Cecil B. DeMille
One of the most successful filmmakers in Hollywood history, DeMille was also one of the first movie directors to become a celebrity in his own right. He is best known for directing such biblical epics as *The Ten Commandments* (1923 and 1956), *The King of Kings* (1927), and *Samson and Delilah* (1949). Known for his flamboyant showmanship, he appeared in several films and won an Academy Award. The Golden Globe Lifetime Achievement Award is named for him. The son of an Episcopal lay reader, he attended St. Stephen's in Hollywood from time to time. His funeral was held there in 1961. DeMille made generous contributions to the parish, including the loan of the marble tablets from *The Ten Commandments*, which graced the church's narthex for many years.

10 David Hyde Pierce
He is best known for his performances on the long-running hit television sitcom *Frazier*. Pierce spent 11 years on the program in the role of Dr. Niles Crane, for which he won four Emmy Awards. His film credits include *Little Man Tate* (1991), *Sleepless in Seattle* (1993), and *Down with Love* (2003). Pierce is also a talented stage performer and singer, winning a Tony Award in 2007 for his performance in the Broadway musical

Curtains. Growing up in Saratoga Springs, New York, Pierce spent time on the organ bench at his parish, Bethesda Episcopal Church, which is known for its outstanding music program. Pierce is an active supporter of Alzheimer's research, AIDS charities, and lesbian, gay, bisexual, and transgender causes. He has not spoken often about his personal life, including his religion, saying, "I live my life as an open book. I just don't intend to read it to anyone."

TEN FAMOUS HYMNS WRITTEN BY EPISCOPALIANS OR ANGLICANS

You may never hear Casey Kasem or Ryan Seacrest count 'em down, but Episcopalians have their own "Top Ten." In fact, much of the church world is thankful for these dedicated musicians and their contributions to Christian hymnody. If you don't recognize these by name, hop online to *www.cyberhymnal.org,* which will allow you to hear them (albeit not in the way they were originally intended to be heard), and you may be surprised at how many you recognize:

10. "Come, My Way, My Truth, My Life" (text: George Herbert)

9. "I Sing a Song of the Saints of God" (text: Lesbia Scott)

8. "O Love of God, How Strong and True" (text: Horatius Bonar)

7. "We Know that Christ is Raised" (tune: Charles Villiers Stanford)

6. "For All the Saints" (tune: Ralph Vaughn Williams)

5. "O Praise Ye the Lord" (tune: Charles Hubert Hastings Parry)

4. "Praise My Soul the King of Heaven" (tune: John Goss)

3. "Hail Thee, Festival Day" (tune: Ralph Vaughan Williams)

2. "The Church's One Foundation" (tune: Samuel Sebastian Wesley)

1. "Amazing Grace" (text: John Newton)

Of course, this is not a definitive list, and the rankings are purely subjective. But it is an introduction to a cherished and much-appreciated repertoire that has helped Episcopalians do what we love most: worship the Lord.

FIVE FAMOUS EPISCOPALIAN AND ANGLICAN SCIENTISTS

1 **Margaret Mead**

A cultural anthropologist and well-known writer and speaker in the 1960s and 1970s, Margaret Mead may be best known for her controversial book *Coming of Age in Samoa* (1928). Following graduate work at Columbia University, she spent many years working with the American Museum of Natural History in New York City. Her fieldwork in the South Pacific led her to report about the purportedly healthy attitude toward sex in traditional cultures there. A devout Anglo-Catholic and regular churchgoer, she played a considerable role in drafting the 1979 Book of Common Prayer. Mead was a convert to the Episcopal Church and once said, "What I wanted was a form of religion that gave expression to an already existing faith." Among her many accolades was the Presidential Medal of Freedom, awarded posthumously.

2 **Isaac Newton**

This famous physicist, mathematician, and astronomer was one of the most influential scientists who ever lived. Newton's theory of universal gravitation and three laws of motion laid the foundation for modern engineering. He is co-credited with the development of calculus and invented the first practical reflecting telescope. Newton was born into the Church of England and publicly conformed to it, though he held some rather unorthodox views, especially pertaining to the Trinity. Newton also wrote extensively about religion and believed that numbers are deeply involved with understanding God and the Bible. A devoutly religious man, he once wrote, "The most beautiful system of the sun, planets and comets, could only proceed from the counsel and dominion of an intelligent and powerful Being." Isaac Newton died in 1727 and is buried in Westminster Abbey, an Anglican church, and is the first scientist to be accorded that honor.

❸ Jeannette Piccard

A woman of many talents, Piccard was an accomplished scientist, teacher, priest and aeronaut. A member of the renowned Piccard family of balloonists, in 1934 she became the first pilot — and the first woman — to reach the stratosphere (57,579 feet). Jeannette worked on several high-profile balloon projects alongside her husband, scientist Jean Piccard. Both are credited with the invention of the plastic balloon. Jeannette's life-long dream, however, was to become a priest. In 1974, at age 79, she made history as one of the Philadelphia 11 — the first women to be ordained priests in the Episcopal Church. Piccard served congregations in Minnesota until her death at age 86.

❹ Charles Darwin

Some people may find it rather puzzling that the man credited with developing the theory of evolution had a deeply Christian background. As a young man, English naturalist Charles Darwin attended a Church of England school and actually studied Anglican theology with the intent of becoming a clergyman. This was before his famous, five-year journey on the *Beagle,* which led to his theory of natural selection — that all species of life evolved over time from common ancestors — later published in his famous book, *On the Origin of Species.* Later in life, after the death of his daughter,

Darwin's views became much more Unitarian, though he thought of himself not as an atheist but an agnostic. His accomplishments were marked by the church of his birth with his interment at Westminster Abbey, not far from Isaac Newton's grave.

❺ Donald W. Douglas, Sr.
If you've ever flown in a DC-10 passenger plane, you now know what the "D" stands for. Douglas was an aeronautics pioneer and founder of the Douglas Company that built the first airplane to lift a useful load exceeding its own weight. An outstanding student, Douglas graduated from Trinity Chapel School in New York City. He completed his four-year degree at MIT in two years and become an assistant professor in aeronautics there. After founding his own company in 1921, he secured military contracts and designed transport planes, finally launching one of the world's first commercial jetliners, the DC-8, in 1958. His company eventually merged with McDonnell Aircraft, then with Boeing. Douglas was not an outwardly religious man, though his innovative work helped millions of people soar above the heavens. Following his death, his ashes were scattered over the Pacific Ocean.

EPISCOPAL CHURCH SNAPSHOT

The Episcopal Church

- 7,200 congregations

- Average Sunday attendance at a "typical" parish — 129 people

- 2.3 million members

- 52% of churches built before 1950

- One of the 44 national and regional churches that make up the Anglican Communion (80 million members)

- Clergy are male and female

- Clergy are called deacons, priests, and bishops

- Male priests are called "Father" or The Rev.

- Female priests are called "Mother" or The Rev.

- The word "Episcopal" is an adjective, as in "The Episcopal Church." The word "Episcopalian" is a noun. A person is an Episcopalian, but does not attend an Episcopalian Church.

Provinces
of the
Episcopal Church

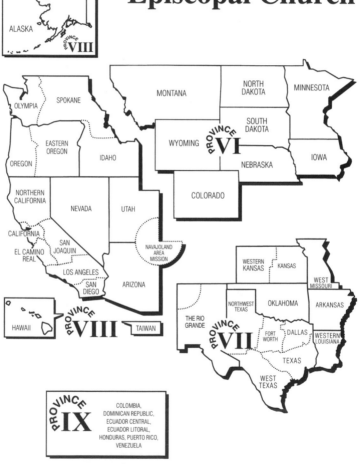

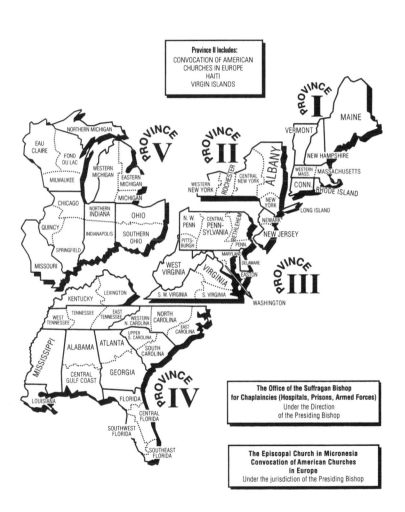

Province II Includes:
CONVOCATION OF AMERICAN
CHURCHES IN EUROPE
HAITI
VIRGIN ISLANDS

PROVINCE I

MAINE

VERMONT

NEW HAMPSHIRE

WESTERN
MASS. MASSACHUSETTS

CONN.

RHODE ISLAND

PROVINCE V

NORTHERN MICHIGAN

EAU
CLAIRE

FOND
DU LAC

WESTERN
MICHIGAN

EASTERN
MICHIGAN

MILWAUKEE

CHICAGO

NORTHERN
INDIANA

MICHIGAN

OHIO

QUINCY

INDIANAPOLIS

SOUTHERN
OHIO

SPRINGFIELD

MISSOURI

PROVINCE II

WESTERN
NEW YORK

ROCHESTER

CENTRAL
NEW YORK

ALBANY

NEW
YORK

LONG ISLAND

NEWARK

NEW JERSEY

N. W.
PENN

CENTRAL
PENN-
SYLVANIA

BETHLEHEM

PITTS-
BURGH

PENN.

MARYLAND

DELAWARE

EASTON

PROVINCE III

WEST
VIRGINIA

VIRGINIA

WASHINGTON

KENTUCKY

LEXINGTON

S. W. VIRGINIA

S. VIRGINIA

TENNESSEE

EAST
TENNESSEE

WESTERN
N. CAROLINA

NORTH
CAROLINA

EAST
CAROLINA

WEST
TENNESSEE

UPPER
S. CAROLINA

MISSISSIPPI

ALABAMA

ATLANTA

SOUTH
CAROLINA

CENTRAL
GULF COAST

GEORGIA

PROVINCE IV

LOUISIANA

FLORIDA

CENTRAL
FLORIDA

SOUTHWEST
FLORIDA

SOUTHEAST
FLORIDA

**The Office of the Suffragan Bishop
for Chaplaincies (Hospitals, Prisons, Armed Forces)**
Under the Direction
of the Presiding Bishop

**The Episcopal Church in Micronesia
Convocation of American Churches
in Europe**
Under the jurisdiction of the Presiding Bishop

EVERYDAY STUFF

HOW TO CARE FOR THE SICK

While a trained and licensed physician must be sought to treat illness and injury, there is no malady that cannot be helped with faithful attention and prayer.

❶ Assess the nature of the problem.
Visit a local pharmacy if the illness is a simple one. Over-the-counter medications usually provide temporary relief until the body heals itself. If symptoms persist, the sick person should see a doctor and get a more detailed diagnosis.

❷ Pray for them.
Intercessory prayers are prayers made on someone else's behalf. Recent studies point to healing in hospitalized patients who have been prayed for — even when the sick were not aware of the prayers. Add the afflicted person to your church's prayer list.

❸ Call in the elders.
Prayer and emotional support from friends and family are vital parts of healing, living with illness, and facing death. Ask the pastor to assemble the church elders (leaders) for prayer and the laying on of hands.

Here's what the Bible says on this topic: "Are any among you sick? They should call for the elders of the church and have them pray over them, anointing them with oil in the name of the Lord" (James 5:14).

Be Aware

* Many people claim expertise in healing, from acupuncturists and herbalists to "faith healers" and psychics. Use caution and skepticism, but keep an open mind.

- Many people believe that much healing can be found in "comfort foods," such as homemade chicken soup.

- Those who attempt to diagnose and treat their own symptoms can often do more harm than good. When in doubt, always consult a pharmacist, doctor, or other medical professional.

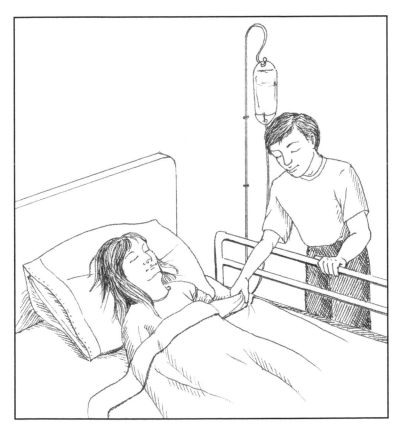

HOW TO CONSOLE A GRIEVING FRIEND

Consolation is a gift from God. Christians in turn give it to others to build up the body of Christ and preserve it in times of trouble. (See 2 Corinthians 1:4–7.) Episcopalians often employ food as a helpful secondary means.

1 Listen first.
Make it known that you're present and available. When the person opens up, be quiet and attentive.

2 Be ready to help the person face grief and sadness, not avoid them.
The object is to help the person name, understand, and work through his or her feelings, not gloss over them.

3 Avoid saying things to make yourself feel better.
"I know exactly how you feel," is seldom true and trivializes the sufferer's pain. Even if you have experienced something similar, no experience is exactly the same. If there is nothing to say, simply be present with the person.

4 Show respect with honesty.
Don't try to answer the mysteries of the universe or force your beliefs on the person. Be clear about the limitations of your abilities. Be ready to let some questions go unanswered. Consolation isn't about having all the answers, it's about bearing one another's burdens.

5 Don't put words in God's mouth.
Avoid saying, "This is God's will," or, "This is part of God's plan." Unless you heard it straight from God, don't say it.

HOW TO COPE
WITH LOSS AND GRIEF

Episcopalians tend to downplay their losses by saying, "Oh, I'm fine, thanks." This may provide only temporary relief at best. Any loss can cause pain, feelings of confusion, and uncertainty. These responses are normal.

❶ Familiarize yourself with the stages of grief.
Experts identify five: denial, anger, bargaining, depression, and acceptance. Some add hope as a sixth stage. Grieving persons cycle back and forth through the stages, sometimes experiencing two or three in a single day. This is normal.

❷ Express your grief.
Healthy ways may include crying, staring into space for extended periods, ruminating, shouting at the ceiling, and sudden napping. Laughing outbursts are also appropriate and should not be judged harshly.

❸ Identify someone you trust to talk to.
Available people can include a spouse, parents, relatives, friends, a pastor, a doctor, or a trained counselor. Many household pets also make good listeners and willing confidants.

❹ Choose a personal way to memorialize the loss.
Make a collage of photographs, offer a memorial donation to your church, or start a scrapbook of memories to honor the event. This helps you to begin to heal without getting stuck in your grief.

Be Aware

- Many experts prescribe a self-giving activity, such as volunteering at a shelter or soup kitchen, as a means of facilitating a healthy grieving process.

- The pain immediately after suffering a loss is usually deep and intense. This will lessen with the passage of time.

- Anger, guilt, bitterness, and sadness are likely emotions.

- Short-term depression may occur in extreme cases. After experiencing a great loss, such as the death of a loved one, make an appointment with your family physician for a physical.

- Even Jesus cried when his friend Lazarus died (John 11:35).

Even Jesus felt the loss of Lazarus when he died.

Mary

Martha

HOW TO FORGIVE SOMEONE

Forgiving is one of the most difficult disciplines of faith, since it seems to cost you something additional when you've already been wronged. Swallowing your pride and seeking a greater good, however, can yield great healing and growth.

❶ Acknowledge that God forgives you.
When you realize that God has already shown forgiveness, and continues to forgive sinners like you, it's easier to forgive someone else.

❷ Consult Scripture.
Jesus taught the Lord's Prayer to his disciples, who were hungry to become like he was. Forgiveness was a big part of this. Read Matthew 6:9–15.

❸ Seek the person out whenever possible.
Consciously decide to deliver your forgiveness in person. In cases where this is geographically impossible, find an appropriate alternative means, such as the telephone.

Note: This may not be wise in all cases, given the timing of the situation or the level of hurt. Certain problems can be made worse by an unwelcome declaration of forgiveness. Consult with a clergyperson before taking questionable action.

❹ Say, "I forgive you," out loud.
A verbal declaration of forgiveness is ideal. Speaking the words enacts a physical chain reaction that can create healing for both speaker and hearer. In the Bible, Jesus used these words to heal a paralyzed man from across a room.

❺ Pray for the power to forgive.
Praying for this is always good, whether a forgiveness situation is at hand or not. It is especially helpful in cases where declaring forgiveness seems beyond your reach.

Be Aware

• When someone sins against you personally, forgiving them does NOT depend upon them feeling sorry (showing contrition) or asking for your forgiveness. But it helps. You may have to struggle, however, to forgive them without their consent or participation.

HOW TO PRAY

Prayer is intimate communication with God and can be used before a meal, at bedtime, during a worship service, or any time the need or opportunity arises. Silent and spoken prayers are both okay and may be used liberally throughout the day. Prayer is also taking time to listen to what God is saying to us. Spontaneous prayer is often best, but the following process may help build the habit.

1 **Assess your need for prayer.**
Take stock of the situation at hand, including your motivations. What are you praying *for* and why?

2 **Select a type of prayer.**
Prayers of *supplication* (requests for God's help), *contrition* (in which sin is confessed and forgiveness requested), *intercession* (on behalf of others), and others are good and time tested. The Book of Common Prayer, books of personal prayers, hymnals, and devotionals often contain helpful, prewritten prayers. Consider also an ad-libbed prayer from the heart.

3 **Select a physical prayer posture.**
Many postures are appropriate:

- The most common type of prayer in the New Testament is from a prone position, lying face-down on the ground, arms spread.

- Kneeling with your face and palms upturned is good for prayers of supplication.

- Bowed head with closed eyes and hands folded is common today and aids concentration.

There is no "official" posture for prayer. Choose your posture according to your individual prayer needs.

4 **Offer your prayer.**

Pray with confidence. God listens to all prayer and responds. Breathe deeply, relax, and be open as the Spirit leads you.

5 **Listen.**

Take time during your prayer simply to listen. Some prayer traditions involve only silent meditation as a means of listening for God's voice.

Be Aware

◆ God hears every prayer.

◆ Prayer can be done either alone or in the company of others (corporately).

◆ Environment matters. If possible, consider lighting a candle and dimming the lights to set the correct mood and help block out distractions.

Choose a comfortable and appropriate prayer posture for your prayer time.

HOW TO RESOLVE INTERPERSONAL CONFLICT

Disagreements are part of life. They often occur when we forget that not everyone sees things the same way. Conflict should be viewed as an opportunity to grow, not a contest for domination. Episcopalians can be rather reserved, but when push comes to shove they value healthy relationships above all.

1 Adopt a healthy attitude.
Your frame of mind is critical. Approach the situation with forethought and calm. Prayer can be invaluable at this stage. Do not approach the other party when you're angry or upset.

2 Read Matthew 18:15–20 beforehand.
Consult the Bible to orient your thinking. This is the model Jesus provided and can be used to call to mind an appropriate method.

3 Talk directly to the person involved.
Avoid "triangulation." Talking about someone to a third party can make the conflict worse, as the person may feel that he or she is the subject of gossip. Speaking with the other person directly eliminates the danger and boosts the odds of a good outcome.

4 Express yourself without attacking.
Using "I statements" can avoid casting the other person as the "bad guy" and inflaming the conflict. "I statements" are sentences beginning with phrases such as "I feel . . . " or "I'm uncomfortable when . . . "

5 **Keep "speaking the truth in love" (Ephesians 4:15) as your goal.**

Your "truth" may not be the other party's. Your objective is to discover and honor each other's "truth," not to put down the other person. Be ready to admit your own faults and mistakes.

6 **Seek out a third party to act as an impartial witness.**
If direct conversation doesn't resolve the conflict, locate someone both parties trust to sit in. This can help clarify your positions and bring understanding.

7 **Build toward forgiveness and a renewed friendship.**

Agree upon how you will communicate to prevent future misunderstandings.

Be Aware

- Seemingly unrelated events in your or the other person's life may be playing an invisible role in the conflict at hand. Be ready to shift the focus to the real cause.

- You may not be able to resolve the conflict at this time, but don't give up on future opportunities.

HOW TO WORK
FOR WORLD PEACE

Like many Christians, Episcopalians have a passion for bringing Christ's peace into the world. These days clergy and lay people are working hand in hand on some exciting and important projects. Here are just a few of them:

The Office for Peace and Justice Ministries of the Episcopal Church coordinates ministries we use to carry out the promises we make in our Baptismal Covenant (see page 228), specifically to "strive for peace and justice and respect the dignity of every human being." Peace and Justice concentrates on six areas: social justice, Jubilee ministry, government relations, criminal justice, environmental stewardship, and peace ministries. Check them out at *www.episcopalchurch.org/peace_justice.htm*.

Episcopalians for Global Reconciliation is a relatively young, grassroots organization serving as a clearinghouse for relevant and practical information on improving the world. This group routinely organizes fund drives and special events to involve Episcopalians and their parishes in their ongoing work. Sign up for their e-newsletter at *www.e4gr.org*.

The United Thank Offering has been lobbying the church on behalf of the poor since 1889. Their little blue boxes are passed out each year to collect the loose change that results in millions of dollars of grants (*www.episcopalchurch.org/uto*). Thousands of projects around the world have benefited from the money Episcopalians donate to this important work.

WHAT ARE THE MILLENNIUM DEVELOPMENT GOALS?

They're life-saving, world-changing, and, most importantly, doable.

The eight Millennium Development Goals (MDGs) were set by the United Nations in 2000. They're tangible targets to make significant progress in solving the world's most pressing problems by the year 2015. One hundred eighty-nine nations have signed on (including the United States). The MDGs are:

Goal 1: Eradicate extreme poverty and hunger

Goal 2: Achieve universal primary education

Goal 3: Promote gender equality and empower women

Goal 4: Reduce child mortality

Goal 5: Improve maternal health

Goal 6: Combat HIV/AIDS, malaria, and other diseases

Goal 7: Ensure environmental sustainability

Goal 8: Develop a global partnership for development

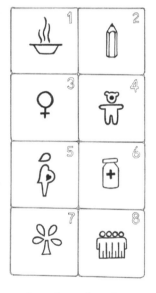

The Episcopal Church is one of many churches that have made the MDGs a priority. Some parishes are partnering by pledging .07% of their budgets toward funding some of these goals. Episcopalians are also actively lobbying our government to do the same thing. Find out more at *www.globalgood.org.*

WHERE TO FIND A TRUSTWORTHY RELIEF AGENCY

We all hear the complaints about nonprofits that spend so much money on overhead and marketing that only pennies on the dollar actually end up going to help the needy.

Episcopalians are proud to say that is not the case with our most prominent aid agency, Episcopal Relief and Development (ERD). For more than 60 years, ERD has served the needs of the poor and vulnerable at home and in 100 countries worldwide. ERD says 92 percent of donated dollars go directly toward field programs. ERD is able to do this because investment income and shared administration costs with the Episcopal Church cover much of the overhead and fundraising costs, which allows donors to know that their gifts, for the most part, go directly to the need. In 2008, ERD was awarded a 4-star rating from Charity Navigator for its sound fiscal management.

From a practical point of view, churches are often the best ways to help in time of disaster. Unlike other agencies that may not have strong ties to an area, churches already have buildings and established relationships with those affected so that, often times. many more resources can be spent directly on those most in need.

ERD has 3,000 volunteers in its network who donate time in a variety of ways. If you have disaster expertise and would like to pitch in here or overseas, contact ERD at *www.er-d.org*.

HOW TO GO TO HEAVEN IF YOU'RE RICH

Episcopalians aren't the only ones who wonder about this — it's something every American Christian needs to consider. After all, Americans make up five percent of the world's population yet use 30 percent of its resources. We live in the richest country that's ever existed. While much of the world dies of starvation, our biggest health problem is obesity. And this is bound to raise important questions about our religion. After all, Jesus talked a lot about money.

Believe it or not, next to the Kingdom of God, money is the most frequent topic Jesus discussed. In the New Testament, one in every 16 verses deals with the subjects of poverty, wealth, injustice, oppression and God's response to these. In the first three Gospels, it's one in every ten verses. In the book of Luke, it's one in seven. What's more, Jesus didn't speak too highly of those who had a lot of money. The Rich Young Ruler mentioned in Matthew is the only person mentioned in the Bible who refused to take Jesus up on his invitation to "follow me": "When the young man heard this word he went away grieving, for he had many possessions." (Matthew 19:22)

We all know that money has an alluring and enticing side, one that can so excite us with possessions and experiences that we unwittingly turn a blind eye to our responsibilities to the poor. Money and possessions can become idols and false gods. This is not to say that Christians cannot (or should not) be rich. Money is not inherently bad, but it is dangerous. Those who have much are responsible for sharing it with those who have little. There is enough money in the world for everyone's need, but not for everyone's greed. Going to heaven, then, may not depend so much on how much we have, as how much we share.

HOW EPISCOPALIANS LOBBY CONGRESS

You mean the Episcopal Church is involved in politics?

Of course, and we have been for quite a while. Like many Christian bodies, the Episcopal Church has an established presence in Washington, DC, in the form of the Office of Government Relations and the Episcopal Public Policy Network (EPPN). The EPPN is made up of some 20,000 Episcopalians from around the country who bring the positions of the Episcopal Church to our nation's lawmakers. The social policies established by General Convention and Executive Council include areas like international peace and justice, human rights, immigration, welfare, poverty, violence and much more.

The Office of Government Relations staff meets regularly with government leaders, works with media, and forms both religious and secular coalitions to further the Church's social policies. Episcopalians establish these policies when we gather every three years in Convention. This is when we pass resolutions urging action in a number of different areas, like increasing aid to war-torn areas of Africa or urging disarmament of nuclear weapons.

EPPN sees its work as an extension of our Baptismal Covenant (see page 228) as we strive for justice and peace among all people. You can learn more (and join!) by contacting them at *www.episcopalchurch.org/eppn.*

HOW EPISCOPALIANS EVANGELIZE

In Episcopal circles it is known as the dreaded "E" word.

Perhaps it's because many of us come from backgrounds where "evangelism" and "evangelical" have left sour tastes in our mouths. Episcopalians have nothing against sharing our faith with others; it's just that we tend to do it differently than those who are more vocal about it.

Episcopalians understand that sharing our faith is not optional, it's a long-standing biblical command, and it's something we take very seriously. Episcopalians tend to see their evangelism as something much deeper than simply making converts (see page 136). That's why we tend to shy away from emotion-charged services that can be interpreted as high-powered sales pitches. We see salvation as a journey and a process, not a one-time event. A former archbishop of Canterbury was once asked, "Are you saved?" to which he replied, "I was saved, I am being saved, and I will be saved."

Many Episcopalians link evangelism with the two commandments Jesus gave us, to love God and to love our neighbors. We believe that in loving our neighbor, Christ is revealed. And the Bible says that when Christ is lifted up, he will cause all people to come unto him (John 12:32). That's why Episcopalians tend to be rather laid back when it comes to faith-sharing. We know that the one who really does the work is the Lord. Therefore, our most successful strategy involves being ourselves, loving people, listening to them, praying for them, and being whatever help we can. It means being a friend and family to those around us.

This is why many Episcopal churches open their doors to recovery and community groups, like Alcoholics Anonymous or the Kiwanis Club. We see these as small acts of evangelism and the sharing of Christ's love with others. The hospitality, open-mindedness, and welcome that Episcopalians try to embody is our deepest expression of evangelism. And we believe this is what truly resonates with those who are searching for God.

Sharing God by loving others is at the heart of how Episcopalians evangelize.

HOW EPISCOPALIANS MAKE DISCIPLES

One of the last things Jesus told those who would follow him was this: "Go therefore and make disciples of all nations." (Matthew 28:1) Jesus seemed intent on having Christians go forward and not simply tell people who he was, but to bring people to a deeper understanding and imitation of Christ.

Many different churches do this in many different ways. Episcopalians do it through worship. Since worship is all about engaging in the endless work of giving thanks, this is a holistic task that involves everything we are. Episcopal worship revolves around regular times of prayer and culminates in our Sunday celebration of Holy Eucharist. During the week, the Book of Common Prayer recommends we give thanks to God at Morning Prayer (BCP, page 75) and Evening Prayer (BCP, page 115). There are other opportunities for worship at other times of the day (noon, at meals, and before bed) that are also included in the Prayer Book (see page 251). All are designed to help us be the thankful, generous-hearted and Christ-centered people we want to be.

At Sunday worship, we engage in the work of discipleship by coming together to hear the Bible proclaimed and interpreted, and by taking part in that mystical and mysterious ritual of Holy Communion. This was the most profound act of worship Jesus taught his disciples. On the night before he died, Jesus took bread and broke it, then took wine and shared it, symbolic of how he was to give himself for us. When we partake of this meal we are reminded of how we too break open our lives and pour them out in love to a hurting world. It's all about imitating Christ and serving God by serving the world, which is the essence of discipleship.

WHY (SOME OF) OUR CHURCH DOORS ARE RED

Some call it tradition; others think it's just a snappy looking color. But the deeper reason belongs to our firm belief that our churches are refuges.

Like many churches, Episcopal parishes use red to let the world know what we're about. Red is the color of Christ's blood. It is the symbol of the sacrifice of the martyrs. It is the presence of the Holy Spirit. And it marks the holy ground that lies just beyond its doors. We like to think that red tells the world we're a safe place. We're a peaceful place. We're a place of refuge.

Historically, churches painted their doors red to signal fleeing suspects that they were places of asylum (thank King Ethelbert's English law, circa 600 C.E.). Today we know that the world is a scary place, full of people who are looking for places to find peace and forgiveness. While many people look at traditional churches as daunting and inhospitable (ever notice how many church doors are locked these days?) we hope that our red doors tell a different story.

Most Episcopalians are converts (see page 77) and many have had bad church experiences that have left them scarred or leery about God and God's people. We know that churches are not so much museums for saints as they are hospitals for sinners. So like hospitals display a red cross, we also like to advertise that we too are a place of healing and restoration. At our best, our parishes help the wounded put their lives back together, provide comfort in time of need, and are open to all who knock.

HOW TO TELL THE DIFFERENCE BETWEEN A SINNER AND A SAINT

Many Christians claim they can tell the difference between saints and sinners. Sinners are naughty and do naughty things, they say, and saints are nice and do nice things. For Episcopalians, however, who strive to seek and serve Christ in all persons, distinguishing saint from sinner has never been easy.

❶ Grapple briefly with the following question: "Can the finite bear the infinite?"
Originally used by the church to help resolve the debate over whether Jesus was all man (completely human) or all God (completely divine), this question can be useful when discerning sinner from saint. Episcopalians answer the question by saying, "Yes!" Baptism makes the finite (you) able to bear the infinite (Christ), so it's not a matter of naughty or nice, sinner or saint (or, in Jesus' case, man or God). A person is fully a saint and fully a sinner at the same time.

❷ Embrace the sinner so that the saint can be revealed. Avoid pulling punches.
Fearlessly and truthfully answer the question, "Am I (or, are you) a sinner?" based strictly on the evidence at hand. (Hint: when in doubt simply measure yourself or the other person against the Ten Commandments.) If you hedge by saying, "No, not totally. I keep some commandments sometimes," you are blissfully deluded.

❸ Bone up on what the Bible says about it.
Scripture makes clear that being a sinner is a prerequisite for being a saint (see Romans 5:8; Galatians 2:17; and Matthew 9:13). Why else would a saint like the apostle Paul "boast" that he was himself the chief of sinners (1 Timothy 1:15)? Why else would he confess that "I do not do the good I want but the evil I do not want is what I do"?

❹ Employ standard Episcopalian "via media" thinking.
On the one hand, people are sinners when they disobey God's Commandments and when they doubt or disbelieve the Word of God. The end of such sinners is death. On the other hand, people are saints when they are justified by faith in Christ and when they continue to trust and believe God's promises in Christ. The end of such saints is eternal life.

Be Aware

◆ Although Christians are exhorted to "tame the flesh," they can't make themselves "less of a sinner" over time. You can't become, say, 35 percent sinner and 65 percent saint if you just work really hard at it. You can't change the percentages of sinner/saint within you.

FIVE IMPORTANT EPISCOPAL MISSIONARIES AND WHAT THEY DID

1 **Jonathan Daniels**

A seminary student from New England, Daniels was a missionary to blacks in the South who were fighting for equal rights. In 1965, Daniels was among those responding to Martin Luther King, Jr.'s call to protest in Alabama, when he was shot outside a grocery store while protecting an African-American teen. His death, at age 26, helped awaken Americans to the seriousness of the civil rights challenge in the United States.

2 **Jackson Kemper**

The first missionary bishop of the Episcopal Church, Kemper left his native New York to found missions in the Midwest. In 1835, Kemper headed west to found, among other things, a college in St. Louis, Missouri, a seminary in Racine, Wisconsin, and a mission parish in Milwaukee that stands today as the Cathedral Church of All Saints.

3 **Thomas Gallaudet**

Known as a missionary to the deaf, Gallaudet carried on a family tradition. The son of Thomas H. Gallaudet, who helped found the first institution for the education of the deaf in North America, young Thomas founded a church and school for the deaf. One of his students, Henry Winter Syle, became the first deaf person ordained in the Episcopal Church.

4 **David Pendleton Oakerhater**
An American Indian, Oakerhater was a warrior and leader of the Cheyenne Indians in Oklahoma. Following his capture and conversion to Christianity while incarcerated, Oakerhater became a deacon and then returned to his native land. As a missionary to the Cheyenne in the 1930s, Oakerhater founded several schools and missions.

5 **Caroline Louise Darling**
Better known by her Christian name, Sister Constance, she was a nineteenth-century missionary to those struck by yellow fever. Constance and several others moved to Memphis, Tennessee, during the epidemics, as droves of people were moving out. In 1878, when an epidemic killed more than 5,000 people, Constance, three other nuns, and two priests were also fatally stricken with the disease.

HOW TO BECOME A MISSIONARY (SHORT-TERM)

Adventure, intrigue, and service — there are plenty of reasons people choose to help others through work on the short-term mission field.

The Episcopal Church offers numerous opportunities for short-term (six months to two years) missions. Through its Volunteers for Mission program, volunteers are placed throughout the world based on requests from bishops throughout the 500-plus dioceses of the Anglican Communion (see page 144). These positions can be domestic or international. Through the Young Adult Service Corps, assignments are typically one year and offer a component of guided reflection and mentoring.

Volunteers might work as teachers in music, English, math, or theology. They also may work providing supervision in homes for young girls, as building project foremen and forewomen, serve as community development workers, set up computer networks and financial management systems, and much more.

The Episcopal Church looks for committed Christians who feel called to the task and are physically and mentally strong. Volunteers are usually active in their congregations and dioceses and are eager to work in partnership with others. One's parish and diocese usually provide the financial support.

The first step is to contact your local clergyperson and begin the conversation. You can also go to the Episcopal Church website (*www.episcopalchurch.org*) to get applications and program overviews.

HOW TO BECOME
A MISSIONARY (FOR LIFE)

So you want to make it a career?

Those who serve for three years or longer in the mission field for the Episcopal Church are typically called Appointed Missionaries (or "Appointees"). These folks take on many of the same tasks as short-term missionaries (through the Volunteers in Mission or the Young Adult Service Corps); however, their terms are longer, renewable, and include financial support from the Episcopal Church.

Life in the mission field is not for the faint of heart. Not only does it require the physical and mental strength to deal with separation from a home environment, but it also requires a deep spirituality. This means that the central task of the missionary is to love the people whom you encounter. Missionaries undertake an array of life-giving tasks, but the most important is to show forth Christ's love.

Appointees often have advanced degrees in theology, missiology, or a field related to their work. Their tasks may include medicine, social work, and development. Nearly 100 men and women are currently engaged in mission work of this kind. They see their work of partnering with indigenous people as a way to live out their Baptismal Covenant (see page 228).

If you're interested in finding out more, contact your Episcopal clergyperson to begin the conversation. You can also go the Episcopal Church website (*www.episcopalchurch.org*) and search under "missionworks."

WHAT IS THE ANGLICAN COMMUNION AND HOW CAN I JOIN?

The Episcopal Church is one of 44 national and regional church associations in 166 countries worldwide that make up the Anglican Communion (see page 204). We're more than 80 million members strong, and growing (especially if you join).

We are a rather loosely based confederation held together by Jesus Christ and the distinctive beliefs we share. These are based on the principles of the English Reformation; episcopal government by apostolic succession, a liturgical worship style, and the Bible informed and interpreted by tradition and reason (see page 150). Our spiritual leader is the Archbishop of Canterbury. His headquarters is at Lambeth Palace in London, England. The archbishop is not a pope; he makes no claims to infallibility, and his formal authority is limited to England. Nonetheless, he is considered our spiritual leader and Episcopalians accord him high respect.

The Anglican Communion is the third-largest body of Christians in the world. This means that practically anywhere you go you'll find a church that worships nearly the same way Episcopalians do. All of these churches have Prayer Books, though they are often written and adopted by each local body, adding a richness and distinction reflective of the home culture. Members of one church can easily transfer membership to another, regardless of the country (or continent). Joining the Episcopal Church automatically makes you a member of the Anglican Communion.

TEN BEAUTIFUL EPISCOPAL CHURCHES

Beauty is in the eye of the beholder, of course. Nonetheless, here are ten very different and quite lovely examples of the wide variety of architectural styles as seen in Episcopal churches—one from each province of the Episcopal Church and the Convocation of American Churches in Europe. Look them up online, or visit them if you find yourself nearby.

Province I:
St. Andrew's, Newcastle, Maine

Province II:
Grace Church, Allentown, Pennsylvania

Province III:
St. James' Church, Lothian, Maryland

Province IV:
Holy Trinity, Vicksburg, Mississippi

Province V:
Church of the Atonement, Fish Creek, Wisconsin

Province VI:
Cathedral of Our Merciful Saviour, Faribault, Minnesota

Province VII:
Grace Cathedral, Topeka, Kansas

Province VIII:
Grace Church, Bainbridge Island, Washington

Province IX:
Catedral de el Señor, Quito, Ecuador

Convocation of American Churches in Europe:
Church of the Ascension, Munich, Germany

WHY THE EPISCOPAL CHURCH WELCOMES EVERYONE

Like many Christians, Episcopalians see Jesus' central message as reconciliation — the repairing of relationships between God and creation. When Jesus came to do this work he didn't surround himself with people who had their acts together, like pious rabbis or society's upstanding citizens. Jesus spent an inordinate amount of time hanging out with sinners, prostitutes, tax collectors, lepers, women — basically, society's marginalized and outcast. Jesus famously said that healthy people don't need doctors, sick people do.

Episcopalians take this to heart. We see Jesus' proclivity to invite everyone, and not turn anybody away. We like to think we welcome everyone because Jesus does.

Welcoming everyone does not mean we have no rules, boundaries, or guidelines. What it means is that we tend to be slow to judge and condemn. After all, one of Jesus' harshest warnings was not to judge (Matthew 7:1). Judgment is up to God. And when the verdict comes in, we believe God's mercy will win out over God's judgment. This is why we believe that showing God's acceptance, forgiveness, love, and welcome should be our defining characteristics.

Episcopalians betray their optimism in the very first line of our Catechism (see page 230). When asked "What are we by nature?" our first answer is not, "wormy sinners in the hands of a fire-breathing God," but, "we are part of God's creation, made in the image of God." It's not that Episcopalians dismiss sin (some of us are particularly good at it!), it's that we believe that Jesus' power to overcome human transgressions and bring forgiveness is more powerful. The Gospel of reconciliation makes Episcopalians a hopeful people who love to laugh, celebrate, and welcome everyone to the party, which means you're invited too.

BIBLE STUFF

HOW EPISCOPALIANS READ THE BIBLE (AND WHY MORE SHOULD)

It's the best-selling book of all time — and possibly the least read.

Polls come out annually showing how many Bibles people own (the average American home has four), yet how utterly clueless we are about what's in it. A recent poll says 10 percent of us believe Joan of Arc was Noah's wife. While Episcopalians probably score about average in this category, it's not for lack of exposure, or a definite interpretive model toward understanding the Holy Scriptures.

In general, Episcopalians have two rules when it comes to interpreting the Bible. The first is that we read it together. The second is that we interpret it responsibly. As children of the English Reformation, which brought us the English Bible (you can thank us later), we are strong believers in everyone's ability to read and interpret Scripture. We like to think that the observations of the farmhand, the homemaker, the nurse, and the auto mechanic are integral to arriving at what it is the Scriptures are saying to us.

However, we also believe there is a place for reasoned, informed, and educated opinion on the matter. When we read the Bible we are apt to do so alongside a study book called a commentary. We also think it fitting to hold and attend classes that expose us to the finest Bible scholarship available. And Episcopalians believe in and rely on an educated clergy who go through a minimum three-year graduate divinity program. Parishioners often look to clergy as resources for Bible interpretation.

Despite these convictions, Episcopalians are usually the first ones to admit we're not Bible experts. Many of us think we should read the Bible more often. And many of us are thankful that we have much knowledge at hand should we decide to do so. Although we still wouldn't know who Noah's wife was; the Bible never names her.

WHO WROTE THE BIBLE?

The short answer is: God. The long answer is . . . much longer.

As we all know, the Bible is not a book, but a collection of books — sixty-six (plus the Apocrypha) put together by dozens of authors. These books span more than a thousand years and include many different genres like history, poetry, praise, wisdom, and prophecy. It's no surprise that each book has its own story of authorship and thanks to the black hole of antiquity we simply don't have answers to a lot of important questions.

While many Christians believe a more traditional view — that the Bible was divinely and inerrantly written by the hand of God — Episcopalians tend to see it a bit differently. Many of us view the Bible as the word of God that comes to us through humans. Thus the biases, preferences, and prejudices these authors carried may be, to some degree, present in the final product. There is almost universally agreed-upon evidence of addition and subtraction that has occurred in the compiling of our most sacred book. This does not make the Bible any less "true" but it does help us better understand it.

We do know that the Bible was primarily written by two communities, ancient Israel and the emerging Christian community. The latest scholarship suggests that some books, like the Gospels (Matthew, Mark, Luke, and John), were indeed the products not so much of these individuals, but of the communities to which they were tied. There is no doubt that these holy men and women, moved by God, participated in bringing these great writings to us. So we tend to see the Bible's origins less as a divine product with divine authority and more as a human response to the presence and action of God.

What's more, we believe God is still writing. While we're not about to suggest any additions to the Bible, we are alert to ways the Living God continues to inform us and communicate with us. Our quest for authorship is ongoing, as is our search for the ways God continues to speak and actively move in our lives.

One Episcopal thinker likes to describe the way many of us see the Bible as historical, metaphorical, and sacramental. Historical, meaning it is a product of its time, not written to us or for us, but nonetheless incredibly illuminating. Metaphorical, in that it is more than literal, and more than factual, and we are less concerned with how it happened than what it means. And sacramental, referring to the Bible's ability to mediate the sacred; in other words, how is this book working as a vehicle of the Holy Spirit in our lives?

Episcopalians don't tend to take all of the Bible literally, but we do take it seriously. This includes paying attention to the latest archaeological findings that help us understand the history and origins of the Scriptures.

COMMON TRANSLATIONS OF THE BIBLE

Translation	Grade Level*	Theological Affiliation	Year Released	Special Features
King James Version	12.0	Church of England, conservative and evangelical	1611	Poetic style using Elizabethan English. Most widely used translation for centuries.
New American Standard Bible	11.0	Conservative and evangelical	1971; updated, 1995	Revision of the 1901 American Standard Version into contemporary language.
New Revised Standard Version	8.1	Mainline and interconfessional	1989	Updated version of the Revised Standard Version.
New King James Version	8.0	Transnational, transdenominational, conservative, and evangelical	1982	Updates the King James text into contemporary language.
New International Version	7.8	Transnational, transdenominational, conservative, and evangelical	1978; revised, 1984	Popular modern-language version. Attempts to balance literal and dynamic translation methods.
Today's English Version	7.3	Evangelical and	1976	Noted for its freshness

Version	Grade level*	Classification	Date	Description
New American Bible	6.6	Roman Catholic	1970; revised NT, 1986; revised Psalms, 1991	Official translation of the Roman Catholic Church in the United States.
New Living Translation	6.4	Evangelical	1996	A meaning-for-meaning translation. Successor to the Living Bible.
New Century Version	5.6	Conservative and evangelical	1988; revised, 1991	Follows the *Living Word Vocabulary*.
Contemporary English Version	5.4	Conservative, evangelical, mainline	1995	Easy-to-read English for new Bible readers.
The Message	4.8, from NT samples	Evangelical	2002	An expressive paraphrase of the Bible.

*The grade level on which the text is written, using Dale-chall, Fry, Raygor, and Spache Formulas.

Bible classifications

Apocrypha Bible: Contains certain books that Protestants don't consider canonical. Most of these OT books are accepted by the Roman Catholic Church.

Children's Bible: Includes illustrations and other study aids that are especially helpful for children.

Concordance Bible: Lists places in the Bible where key words are found.

Red Letter Bible: The words spoken by Christ appear in red.

Reference Bible: Pages include references to other Bible passages on the same subject.

Self-Proclaiming Bible: Diacritical marks (as in a dictionary) appear above difficult names and words to help with the pronunciation.

Text Bible: Contains text without footnotes or column references. May include maps, illustrations, and other helpful material.

HOW TO CHOOSE A BIBLE THAT'S RIGHT FOR YOU

Unless you already read biblical Hebrew, Aramaic, and Greek, you need a Bible translation. You could go learn these languages, but someone's already done the work for you. Choose wisely to enjoy a lifetime relationship with the Scriptures.

1 **Examine yourself and your motivations.**
Think about who you are and why you want to explore the Bible. Do you need a simple Bible or a more nuanced translation? Is this Bible for devotional use or for in-depth study? Do you need one with lots of pictures and small words?

2 **Consider a Bible printed in a language you actually speak.**
For example, if thou dost not maketh use of words like dost or maketh, picketh thou another translation.

3 **Seek an actual translation, not a paraphrased version.**
A paraphrase is a rewording of the Bible, an interpretation of a translation. This is like making a photocopy of a photocopy; resolution and clarity start to diminish. Look on the title page or preface for a phrase like "translated from the original languages."

4 **Determine the translation's level of faithfulness to the original wording.**
Look for footnotes offering alternative translations or that point out where the biblical texts are difficult and the meaning uncertain. Translators often make tough choices; good translations clue you in.

5 Read a familiar passage.

Can you understand what you are reading? Does it help you hear God's word anew? Consider a passage other than John 3:16.

6 Clarify your need for "helps."

Does the translation include introductions and explanations by reputable scholars? Such comments are not a part of the Bible, but can be a real plus in understanding the text, especially for serious study. Some study Bibles use call-outs and discussion questions to add another interesting dimension to Scripture reading.

Be Aware

+ Jesus speaks to us through the Bible. Reading an accurate, understandable translation can result in radical life transformations, spiritual maturity, and actual growth in faith.

+ Unless you actually carry your Bible around with you everywhere, do not purchase a nylon cover with zipper and pockets. They're geeky.

Unless you can read biblical Hebrew, Aramaic, and Greek, you might want to find yourself a good translation in a language you understand.

HOW TO READ THE BIBLE

The Bible is a collection of 66 separate books gathered together over hundreds of years and thousands of miles. Divided into the Old Testament (Hebrew language) and the New Testament (Greek language), these writings have many authors and take many forms.

The Bible includes histories, stories, prophecies, poetry, songs, teachings, and laws, to name a few. Christians believe the Bible is the story of God's relationship with humankind and a powerful way that God speaks to people.

❶ Determine your purpose for reading.
Clarify in your own mind what you hope to gain. Your motivations should be well intentioned, such as to seek information, to gain a deeper understanding of God and yourself, or to enrich your faith. Pray for insight before every reading time.

❷ Resolve to read daily.
Commit to a daily regimen of Bible reading. Make it a part of your routine until it becomes an unbreakable habit.

Commit to reading the Bible daily.

❸ Master the mechanics.

- Memorize the books of the Bible in order.

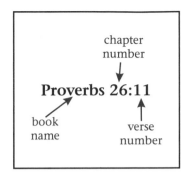

- Familiarize yourself with the introductory material. Many Bible translations include helpful information at the front of the Bible and at the beginning of each book.

- The books are broken down into chapters and verses. Locate the beginning of a book by using the Bible's table of contents. Follow the numerical chapter numbers; these are usually in large type. Verses are likewise numbered in order within each chapter. Simply run your finger down the page until you locate the verse number you're looking for.

- If your Bible contains maps (usually in the back), consult them when cities, mountains, or seas are mentioned in your reading.

❹ Befriend the written text.
Read with a pen or pencil in hand and underline passages of interest. Look up unfamiliar words in a dictionary. Write notes in the margins when necessary. The Bible was written to be read and used, not worshiped.

❺ Practice reading from the Bible out loud.

HOW TO READ THE ENTIRE BIBLE IN ONE YEAR

Reading the entire Bible is a formidable task and can frustrate even the most patient believer when approached willy-nilly. A measured and consistent walk through the Bible, however, can be done without tremendous fuss. Also, when you're finished you can boast that you've read the entire Bible.

1 **Consider purchasing a good "one-year" Bible.** Many good translations are published also in one-year editions. This tool can make the job much easier. It should combine daily Old and New Testament readings with a psalm or section from Proverbs.

2 **Choose a method that matches your personality and reading habits.**

- Start with one book and skip around. Begin with one of the four Gospels, such as John, then read an Old Testament book, like Genesis. Jump to one of the epistles, such as Ephesians. Skipping around keeps your attention fresh.

- Start with the first page and read straight through to the last. This is a common method for Episcopalians, who believe in doing things decently and in order. Keep in mind the first 10 books of the Bible can get fact-heavy and dry. Plowing through them may wear you out fast. If this occurs, try skipping to the juicy parts for variety.

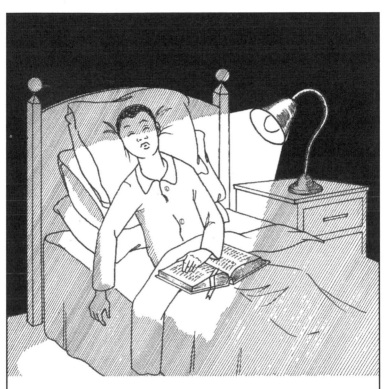

When attempting to read the entire Bible in one year, avoid reading late at night, as this will promote an unwelcome association between God's word and drowsiness.

❸ Covenant with a reading buddy or accountability group.
Commit to each other that you will do your daily readings aloud together when possible and that you'll keep up with them when it's not. Agree to penalties for skipped days.

❹ Celebrate your completed reading of the Bible.
At the end of your Year of the Bible, consider holding a ritual in which you thank God for the experience.

Be Aware

- You do not earn your salvation by reading the Bible, but you will experience growth in faith. Allow the Scriptures to speak to you.

- Many good translations include a suggested one-year reading schedule broken into daily chunks.

- A good bookmark can be almost as important to daily reading as the reading itself. Find one you look forward to seeing each day when you open the book.

- Avoid trying to read as much as you can each sitting. Set limits for yourself or you won't keep your patriarchs straight.

- Avoid reading late at night. Dozing off in the middle of the history books guarantees a later reread.

WHY EPISCOPALIANS HAVE THEIR OWN VERSION OF THE PSALMS

If the Episcopal Church is founded on worship, then it's no surprise that singing plays a very important role. And not just hymn singing, but the singing of the Psalms as well. That's why the Book of Common Prayer contains a unique translation of the Psalms called "The Psalter." It is designed for singing and chanting the Bible's greatest songs in congregational worship.

Of course, Episcopalians did not invent the Psalter. The Hebrews sang the Psalms long before Jesus walked the earth, and there have been several translations down through the ages. However, the unique style and expertise the English brought to the Psalms have probably made the Psalter our most important contribution to Christian literature, after the English Bible and the Book of Common Prayer.

Episcopalians are also the proud inheritors and practitioners of a unique style of singing the Psalms called "Anglican chant." This is the incredibly rich and even breathtaking style of singing often heard by boys' (or girls') choirs in English cathedrals. Developed some five centuries ago, it continues to enrich the worship of countless congregations. More than likely, your local Episcopal parish worships in this style during some portion of the year, and may even offer regular concerts. To find a parish near you, go to *www.theredbook.org.*

DO EPISCOPALIANS BELIEVE IN EVOLUTION?

Some do and some don't. However, what most of us believe in is thoughtful dialogue regarding the role of science in religion.

Many Episcopalians hold to the idea that science and religion are not opposed to one another, but rather are complementary. They both tell us important things about different aspects of reality. They both share the noble mission of discovering truth. In simplistic terms it might be said that science labors to tell us "how," while it is the job of religion to address "why."

Episcopalians find many of our answers in the Bible. That is not to say we are Bible literalists; most of us are not. However it is to say that we hold to the belief found in the Book of Common Prayer that the Bible "contains all things necessary to salvation" (BCP, page 868). It is also to say that the Bible doesn't contain all necessary truths about everything else. The Bible was not written as a science textbook nor do we generally believe it should be used as one. Most of us believe the mystery and complexity of the universe betrays a mysterious and complex God, whom we are still learning.

This means that most Episcopalians tend to be rather curious about the world and how it works. Many of us welcome new scientific discoveries, not because we're contrarians, but because we believe they can shed light on our understandings of God's world and, therefore, God. While the Episcopal Church has never officially spoken on evolution, we have broadly accepted the theory since Darwin's era. (And, Darwin was an Anglican!) Our General Convention has passed a resolution affirming our belief in the ability of God to create in any form and fashion, including evolution.

DOES THE BIBLE CONDEMN GAY PEOPLE?

No more than the Bible condemns straight people.

At issue here is a big question that continues to roil the Church in America — and not just the Episcopal Church. Some Christians believe the Bible's clear, literal interpretation leaves no room for salvation for gay, lesbian, bisexual, and transgendered people. Other Christians, like Episcopalians, not only read these texts differently, but include science, reason, and experience in the conversation and come to a different conclusion.

Like nuclear warfare and stem cell research, there are certain issues that exist today that were simply not around at the time of Jesus. Committed, responsible same-gender relationships are one example. It's true that Jesus never talked about homosexuality, and the texts that do mention it appear condemnatory — but they also leave plenty of room for interpretation. Like many Christians, Episcopalians read these verses keeping in mind the historical context, the perceived audience, and the way these texts fit in with the larger message of the Bible.

And this larger message leads many of us to concentrate on the larger issues facing the world today, like world hunger, desperate poverty, injustice, violence, and war. Yes, Jesus cares who we sleep with, and calls us all to lead pious and holy lives no matter what our sexual orientation. And holy lives are defined by much more than this. The Bible defines them with words like love, joy, peace, patience, generosity, goodness, kindness, and self-control (Galatians 5:22).

Yes, the Bible condemns all who have sinned and fallen short of God's glory, gay and straight. But the Bible also tells us that Jesus redeems all who call upon his name. Episcopalians believe this redemption is open to everybody. As the apostle Paul once put it, "There is no longer Jew or Greek, there is no longer slave or free, there is no longer male and female; for all of you are one in Christ Jesus." (Galatians 3:28)

THE TOP 10 BIBLE HEROES

The Bible is filled with typical examples of heroism, but another kind of hero inhabits the pages of the Bible — those people who, against all odds, follow God no matter the outcome. These are heroes of faith.

❶ Noah

In the face of ridicule from others, Noah trusted God when God chose him to build an ark to save a remnant of humanity from destruction. Noah's trust became part of a covenant with God.

Noah trusted God, even though others made fun of him. By following God's instructions and building a great ark, Noah and his family survived the flood (Genesis 6–10).

❷ Abraham and Sarah

In extreme old age, Abraham and Sarah answered God's call to leave their home and travel to a strange land, where they became the parents of God's people.

❸ Moses

Moses, a man with a speech impediment, challenged the Egyptian powers to deliver God's people from bondage. He led a rebellious and contrary people for 40 years through the wilderness and gave them God's law.

❹ Rahab

A prostitute who helped Israel conquer the promised land, Rahab was the great-grandmother of King David, and thus a part of the family of Jesus himself.

❺ David

Great King David, the youngest and smallest member of his family, defeated great enemies, turning Israel into a world power. He wrote psalms, led armies, and confessed his sins to the Lord.

❻ Mary and Joseph

These humble peasants responded to God's call to be the parents of the Messiah, although the call came through a pregnancy that was not the result of marriage.

❼ The Canaanite Woman

Desperate for her daughter's health, the Canaanite woman challenged Jesus regarding women and race by claiming God's love for all people (Matthew 15:21–28). Because of this, Jesus praised her faith.

❽ Peter

Peter was a man quick to speak but slow to think. At Jesus' trial, Peter denied ever having known him. But in the power of forgiveness and through Christ's appointment, Peter became a leader in the early church.

❾ Saul/Paul

Originally an enemy and persecutor of Christians, Paul experienced a powerful vision of Jesus, converted, and became the greatest missionary the church has ever known.

❿ Phoebe

A contemporary of Paul's, Phoebe is believed to have delivered the book of Romans after traveling some 800 miles from Cenchrea near Corinth to Rome. A wealthy woman, she used her influence to travel, protect other believers, and to host worship services in her home.

Phoebe is believed to have delivered the book of Romans after traveling 800 miles.

THE TOP 10 BIBLE VILLAINS

1 **Satan**
The Evil One is known by many names in the Bible and appears many places, but the devil's purpose is always the same: To disrupt and confuse people so they turn from God and seek to become their own gods. This Bible villain is still active today.

2 **The Serpent**
In Eden, the serpent succeeded in tempting Eve to eat from the tree of the knowledge of good and evil (Genesis 3:1–7). As a result, sin entered creation. If it weren't for the serpent, we'd all still be walking around naked, eating fresh fruit, and living forever.

3 **Pharaoh (probably Seti I or Rameses II)**
The notorious Pharaoh from the book of Exodus enslaved the Israelites. Moses eventually begged him to "Let my people go," but Pharaoh hardened his heart and refused. Ten nasty plagues later, Pharaoh relented, but then changed his mind again. In the end, with his army at the bottom of the sea, Pharaoh finally gave his slaves up to the wilderness.

4 **Goliath**
"The Philistine of Gath," who stood six cubits in height (about nine feet tall), was sent to fight David, still a downy-headed youth of 15. Goliath was a fighting champion known for killing people, but David drilled Goliath in the head with a rock from his sling and gave God the glory (1 Samuel 17).

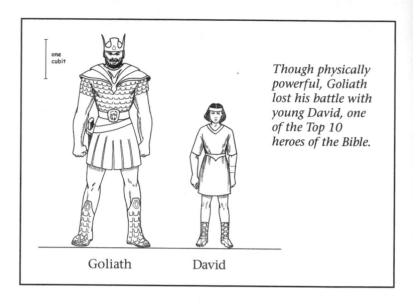

Though physically powerful, Goliath lost his battle with young David, one of the Top 10 heroes of the Bible.

Goliath   David

one cubit

5 Jezebel

King Ahab of Judah's wife and a follower of the false god Baal, Jezebel led her husband away from God and tried to kill off the prophets of the Lord. Elijah the prophet, however, was on the scene. He shamed Jezebel's false prophets and killed them (1 Kings 18:40).

6 King Herod

Afraid of any potential threat to his power, upon hearing about the birth of the Messiah in Bethlehem Herod sent the Wise Men to pinpoint his location. Awestruck by the Savior in the cradle, the Wise Men went home by a different route and avoided Herod. In a rage, he ordered the murder of every child two years of age or younger in the vicinity of Bethlehem. The baby Messiah escaped with his parents to Egypt (Matthew 2:14–15).

❼ The Pharisees, Sadducees, and Scribes

They dogged Jesus throughout his ministry, alternately challenging his authority and being awed by his power. It was their leadership, with the consent and blessing of the people and the Roman government that brought Jesus to trial and execution.

❽ Judas

One of Jesus' original disciples, Judas earned 30 pieces of silver by betraying his Lord over to the authorities. He accomplished this by leading the soldiers into the garden of Gethsemane where he revealed Jesus with a kiss (Matthew 26–27).

❾ Pontius Pilate

The consummate politician, the Roman governor chose to preserve his own bloated status by giving the people what they wanted: Jesus' crucifixion. He washed his hands to signify self-absolution, but bloodied them instead.

❿ God's People

They whine, they sin, they turn their backs on God over and over again. When given freedom, they blow it. When preached repentance by God's prophets, they stone them. When offered a Savior, we kill him. In the end, it must be admitted, God's people — us! — don't really shine. Only by God's grace and the gift of faith in Jesus Christ do we have hope.

THE THREE MOST REBELLIOUS THINGS JESUS DID

1 **The prophet returned to his hometown (Luke 4:14–27).**

Jesus returned to Nazareth, where he was raised and was invited to read Scripture and preach. First, he insisted that the scriptures he read were not just comforting promises of a distant future, but that they were about him, local boy, anointed by God. Second, he insisted God would bless foreigners with those same promises through him. These statements amounted to the unpardonable crime of blasphemy!

2 **The rebel thumbed his nose at the authorities (John 11:55–12:11).**

Jesus had become an outlaw, hunted by the religious authorities who wanted to kill him. Mary, Martha, and Lazarus threw a thank-you party for Jesus in Bethany, right outside Jerusalem, the authorities' stronghold. In spite of the threats to his life, Jesus went to the party. This was not just rebellion but a demonstration of how much Jesus loved his friends.

3 **The king rode a royal procession right under Caesar's nose (Matthew 21:1–17; Mark 11:1–10; Luke 19:28–38; John 12:12–19).**

Jesus entered Jerusalem during a great festival, in full view of adoring crowds, as a king come home to rule. Riding the colt, heralded by the people with cloaks and branches, accompanied by the royal anthem (Psalm 118), he rode in to claim Jerusalem for God and himself as God's anointed. The Roman overlords and the Jewish leaders watched this seditious act and prepared for a crucifixion.

THE FIVE MOST UNPOPULAR OLD TESTAMENT PROPHETS

New Testament tax collectors weren't alone in being hated by God's people. Here are five notorious bearers of God's message and what made them so unpopular.

❶ Amos

Amos gained few friends when he told the Israelites that their privilege came with responsibility. He prophesied against Israel's enemies and then showed Israel's practices were actually worse than the nations they hated. He even said that Israel would be destroyed. Amos let God's people know that God hates violence and oppression of the weak — no matter who's doing it.

❷ Nahum

Nahum told God's people that even a mighty army wouldn't keep a nation safe from God's judgment. About 150 years earlier, Jonah had told the Ninevites to repent (and they did), but they quickly returned to old ways. God gave Nahum a new message of destruction for the Ninevites, but they weren't scared because they had a strong army. So while the city was falling, Nahum ridiculed them by suggesting they draw water (in the midst of a flood), and add bricks to the already demolished city wall.

❸ Micah

Micah told the people that God wants disciples to have humble hearts and behavior that is just and kind to others. He said God would come and destroy the nation of Judah because the powerful had schemed to steal from the poor and followed false prophets. They thought following ritual was enough. It wasn't.

❹ Zephaniah

Zephaniah was another prophet in Judah. He made his enemies by warning that even those who refused to worship idols would face God's judgment because they didn't follow God.

❺ Jeremiah

God called Jeremiah to be a prophet when he was just a boy. This gave him more time to confront God's people about their self-focused lives. He was persecuted bitterly by Judah's last two kings — and even his own extended family tried to kill him. Jeremiah's messages were many — but this one still speaks: Those who are godly may suffer persecution, but they should look to God for salvation!

The Lord's prophets tended to be unpopular, especially among the wealthy, because their messages called for justice toward others and fidelity toward God. Amos was particularly unpopular for this reason.

FIVE INSPIRING WOMEN IN THE BIBLE

There are more than 300 women mentioned in the Bible. Some have names, others are referred to as "the women" or some other similar designation. Theologians and scholars have begun to highlight the lives of these many women and speak of their contributions to the story of God. Here are a few of the more inspiring examples.

1 **Miriam, Jochebed, Puah, Shiphrah, and Pharaoh's daughter**
These five women were instrumental in the survival of Moses. Without their quick thinking, strong courage, and love of God, Moses would have drowned in the Nile River along with many other baby boys. *Note: We are naming more than one woman in this instance, but that's fine. It's a single story that involves them all.*

2 **Ruth**
Ruth chose not to return to her homeland and family after the death of her husband in order to attend to the needs of her mother-in-law, Naomi. Ruth showed intelligence and compassion in gaining the security she and Naomi needed upon their return to Israel. Other women in the story even remarked that Ruth was more valuable than having a son — a high compliment in those days of male preference.

3 **Esther**
When an evil man threatened to annihilate her people, Queen Esther used her beauty and skills in negotiation to save them. Esther is commemorated each year during Purim, a Jewish holiday.

4 **Lydia**

Lydia was known as a God-fearer, a follower of God who regularly prayed with her household. She began a house church and attended to the needs of the apostle Paul. Her house may have been the first European Christian congregation.

5 **Mary, the Mother of the Lord**

At a young age, Mary answered a resounding "YES" to the angel's request that she bear God's Son.

Lydia was a "God fearer," someone who received the gospel of Jesus Christ and was used to spread the good news in her town.

THE TOP 10 BIBLE MIRACLES AND WHAT THEY MEAN

❶ Creation.
God created the universe and everything that is in it, and God continues to create and recreate without ceasing. God's first and ongoing miracle was to reveal that the creation has a purpose.

❷ The Passover.
The Israelites were enslaved by Pharaoh, a ruler who believed the people belonged to him, not to God. In the last of 10 plagues, God visited the houses of all the Egyptians to kill the firstborn male in each one. God alone is Lord of the people, and no human can claim ultimate power over us.

❸ The Exodus.
God's people were fleeing Egypt when Pharaoh dispatched his army to force them back into slavery. The army trapped the people with their backs to a sea, but God parted the water and the people walked across to freedom while Pharaoh's minions were destroyed. God chose to free us from all forms of tyranny so we may use that freedom to serve God and each other.

❹ Manna.
After the people crossed the sea to freedom, they complained that they were going to starve to death. They even asked to go back to Egypt. God sent manna, a form of bread, so the people lived. God cares for us even when we give up, pine for our slavery, and lose faith. God never abandons us.

❺ The Incarnation.
The immortal and infinite God became a human being, choosing to be born of a woman. God loved us enough to become one of us in Jesus of Nazareth, forever bridging the divide that had separated us from God.

❻ Jesus healed the paralyzed man.
Some men brought a paralyzed friend to Jesus. Jesus said, "Son, your sins are forgiven" (Mark 2:5). This means that Jesus has the power to forgive our sins — and he does so as a free gift.

❼ Jesus calmed the storm.
Jesus was asleep in a boat with his disciples when a great storm came up and threatened to sink it. He said, "Peace! Be still!" (Mark 4:39). Then the storm immediately calmed. Jesus is Lord over even the powers of nature.

❽ The Resurrection.
Human beings executed Jesus, but God raised him from the dead on the third day. Through baptism, we share in Jesus' death, so we will also share in eternal life with God the Father, Son, and Holy Spirit. Christ conquered death.

❾ Pentecost.
Jesus ascended from the earth, but he did not leave the church powerless or alone. On the 50th day after the Jewish Passover (Pentecost means 50th), Jesus sent the Holy Spirit to create the church and take up residence among us. The Holy Spirit is present with us always.

❿ The Second Coming.
One day, Christ will come again and end all suffering. This means that the final result of the epic battle between good and evil is already assured. It is simply that evil has not yet admitted defeat.

THE SEVEN FUNNIEST BIBLE STORIES

Humor isn't scarce in the Bible; you just have to look for it. For example, God tells Abraham (100 years old) and Sarah (in her 90s) they'll soon have a son. Understandably, they laugh. Later, they have a son named Isaac, which means "he laughs." Bible humor is also ironic, gross, and sometimes just plain bizarre.

1 **Gideon's dog-men (Judges 6:11–7:23).**
God chooses Gideon to lead an army against the Midianites. Gideon gathers an army of 32,000 men, but this is too many. God tells Gideon to make all the men drink from a stream, and then selects only the 300 men who lap water like dogs.

2 **David ambushes Saul in a cave while he's "busy" (1 Samuel 24:2–7).**
While pursuing David cross-country to engage him in battle, Saul goes into a cave to "relieve himself" (move his bowels). Unbeknownst to Saul, David and his men are already hiding in the very same cave. While Saul's doing his business, David sneaks up and cuts off a corner of Saul's cloak with a knife. Outside afterward, David shows King Saul the piece of cloth to prove he could have killed him "on the throne."

3 **King David does the goofy (2 Samuel 12–23).**
David is so excited about bringing the Ark of the Covenant to Jerusalem that he dances before God and all the people dressed only in a linen ephod, an apron-like garment that covered only the front of his body.

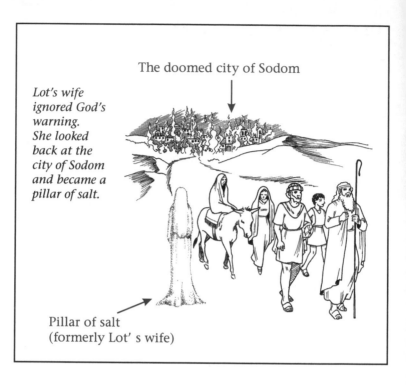

The doomed city of Sodom

Lot's wife ignored God's warning. She looked back at the city of Sodom and became a pillar of salt.

Pillar of salt (formerly Lot's wife)

❹ Lot's wife (Genesis 19:24–26).
While fleeing God's wrath upon the cities of Sodom and Gomorrah, Lot's wife forgets (or ignores) God's warning not to look back upon the destruction and turns into a woman-sized pillar of salt.

❺ Gerasene demoniac (Mark 5:1–20).
A man is possessed by so many demons that chains cannot hold him. Jesus exorcises the demons and sends them into a herd of 2,000 pigs, which then run over the edge of a cliff and drown in the sea. The herders, now 2,000 pigs poorer, get miffed and ask Jesus to leave.

6 **Disciples and loaves of bread** (Mark 8:14–21).
The disciples were there when Jesus fed 5,000 people
with just five loaves of bread and two fish. They also
saw him feed 4,000 people with seven loaves. Later, in
a boat, the disciples fret to an exasperated Jesus because
they have only one loaf for 13 people.

7 **Peter can't swim** (Matthew 14:22–33).
Blundering Peter sees Jesus walking on the water and
wants to join him. But when the wind picks up, Peter
panics and starts to sink. In Greek, the name Peter means
"rock."

*Peter, "the rock,"
sank when he looked
to himself instead of
to Jesus. Jesus later
described Peter as a
Rock of the church
(Matthew 16:18).*

JESUS' TWELVE APOSTLES (PLUS JUDAS AND PAUL)

While Jesus had many disciples (students and followers) the Bible focuses particularly on twelve who were closest to him. Tradition says that these twelve spread Jesus' message throughout the known world (Matthew 28:18–20). For this reason, they were known as apostles, a word that means "sent ones."

❶ Andrew

A fisherman and the first disciple to follow Jesus, Andrew brought his brother, Simon Peter, to Jesus.

❷ Bartholomew

Also called Nathanael, tradition has it that he was martyred by being skinned alive.

❸ James the Elder

James, with John and Peter, was one of Jesus' closest disciples. Herod Agrippa killed James because of his faith, which made him a martyr (Acts 12:2).

❹ John

John (or one of his followers) is thought to be the author of the Gospel of John and three letters of John. He probably died of natural causes in old age.

❺ Matthew

Matthew was a tax collector and, therefore, probably an outcast even among his own people. He is attributed with the authorship of the Gospel of Matthew.

➏ Peter
Peter was a fisherman who was brought to faith by his brother Andrew. He was probably martyred in Rome by being crucified upside down.

➐ Philip
Philip, possibly a Greek, is responsible for bringing Bartholomew (Nathanael) to faith. He is thought to have died in a city called Phrygia.

➑ James the Less
James was called "the Less" so he wouldn't be confused with James, the brother of John, or James, Jesus' brother.

➒ Simon
Simon is often called "the Zealot." Zealots were a political group in Jesus' day that favored the overthrow of the Roman government by force.

➓ Jude
Jude may have worked with Simon the Zealot in Persia (Iran) where they were martyred on the same day.

⑪ Thomas
"Doubting" Thomas preached the message of Jesus in India.

⑫ Matthias
Matthias was chosen by lot to replace Judas. It is thought that he worked mostly in Ethiopia.

⓭ Judas Iscariot

Judas was the treasurer for Jesus' disciples and the one who betrayed Jesus for 30 pieces of silver. According to the Bible, Judas killed himself for his betrayal.

⓮ Paul

Paul is considered primarily responsible for bringing non-Jewish people to faith in Jesus. He traveled extensively and wrote many letters to believers. Many of Paul's letters are included in the New Testament.

THE FIVE BIGGEST MISCONCEPTIONS ABOUT THE BIBLE

❶ The Bible was written in a short period of time.
Christians believe that God inspired the Bible writers, the first of whom may have been Moses. God inspired people to write down important histories, traditions, songs, wise sayings, poetry, and prophetic words. All told — from the first recordings of the stories in Genesis to the last decisions about Revelation — the entire Bible formed over a period spanning anywhere from 800 to 1,400 years!

❷ One person wrote the Bible.
Unlike Islam's Koran, which was written by the prophet Muhammad, the books of the Bible claim the handiwork of many people. Much of Scripture does not identify the human hand that wrote it, so some parts of the Bible may have been written by women as well as men.

❸ The entire Bible should be taken literally.
While many parts of the Bible are meant as descriptions of actual historical events, other parts are intended as illustrations of God's truth, such as Song of Solomon, the book of Revelation, and Jesus' parable of the good Samaritan. So when Jesus says, "If your right eye causes you to sin, tear it out and throw it away" (Matthew 5:29), please do not take the saying literally!

❹ People in Bible times were unenlightened.
During the 1,400 years it took to write the Bible, some of history's greatest thinkers lived and worked. Many of these philosophers, architects, mathematicians, orators, theologians, historians, doctors, military tacticians, inventors, engineers, poets, and playwrights are still quoted today and their works are still in use.

❺ The Bible is a single book.
The Bible is actually a collection of books, letters, and other writings — more like a library than a book. There are 39 books in the Hebrew scriptures, what Christians call the "Old" Testament, and 27 books (mostly letters) in the New Testament. There are seven books in the Apocryhpha (books written between the Old and New Testaments), or "deuterocanonical" books.

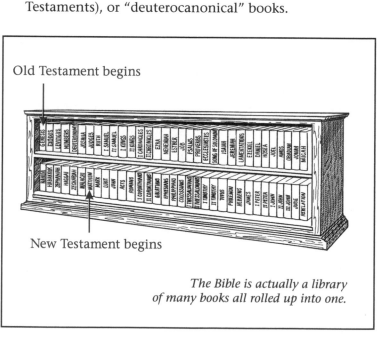

Old Testament begins

New Testament begins

The Bible is actually a library of many books all rolled up into one.

MAPS, DIAGRAMS, CHARTS, AND GLOSSARY

THE EXODUS

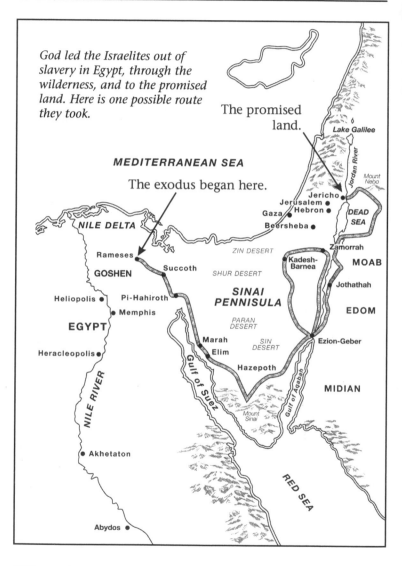

God led the Israelites out of slavery in Egypt, through the wilderness, and to the promised land. Here is one possible route they took.

The promised land.

Lake Galilee

MEDITERRANEAN SEA

The exodus began here.

Jordan River

Mount Nebo

Jericho
Jerusalem
Hebron
Gaza
Beersheba

DEAD SEA

NILE DELTA

Zamorrah

Rameses
Succoth
GOSHEN

ZIN DESERT

Kadesh-Barnea

MOAB

SHUR DESERT

Heliopolis
Pi-Hahiroth
Memphis

SINAI PENNISULA

Jothathah

EGYPT

PARAN DESERT

EDOM

Heracleopolis

Marah
Elim

SIN DESERT

Ezion-Geber

Hazepoth

Gulf of Suez

Gulf of Aqabah

MIDIAN

Akhetaton

Mount Sinai

RED SEA

NILE RIVER

Abydos

THE ARK OF THE COVENANT

*God told the Israelites to place the stone tablets—the "covenant"—
of the law into the Ark of the Covenant. The Israelites believed that
God was invisibly enthroned above the vessel and went before them
wherever they traveled.*

*The Ark of the Covenant was
2.5 cubits long and 1.5 cubits wide
(Exodus 25:17).*

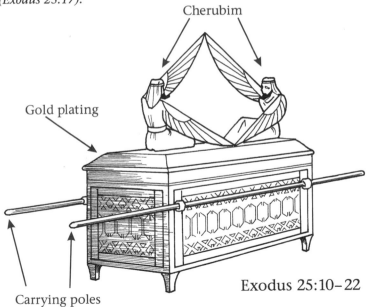

Cherubim

Gold plating

Exodus 25:10–22

Carrying poles

JERUSALEM IN JESUS' TIME

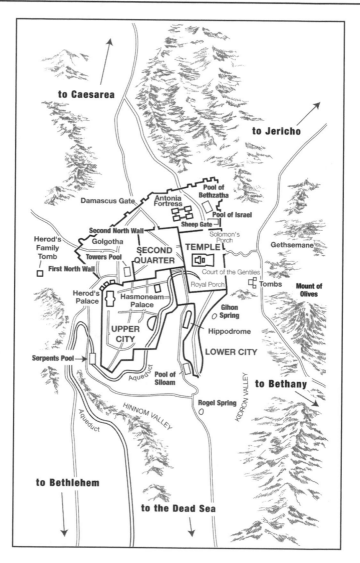

to Caesarea

to Jericho

Pool of Bethzatha

Damascus Gate

Antonia Fortress

Pool of Israel

Second North Wall

Sheep Gate

Solomon's Porch

Herod's Family Tomb

Golgotha

SECOND QUARTER

TEMPLE

Gethsemane

Towers Pool

First North Wall

Court of the Gentiles

Royal Porch

Tombs

Mount of Olives

Herod's Palace

Hasmoneam Palace

Gihon Spring

UPPER CITY

Hippodrome

LOWER CITY

Serpents Pool

Aqueduct

Pool of Siloam

to Bethany

HINNOM VALLEY

Rogel Spring

KIDRON VALLEY

Aqueduct

to Bethlehem

to the Dead Sea

THE PASSION AND CRUCIFIXION

Judas betrayed Jesus with a kiss, saying, "The one I will kiss is the man; arrest him" (Matthew 26:48).

Peter denied Jesus three times (Matthew 26:69–75).

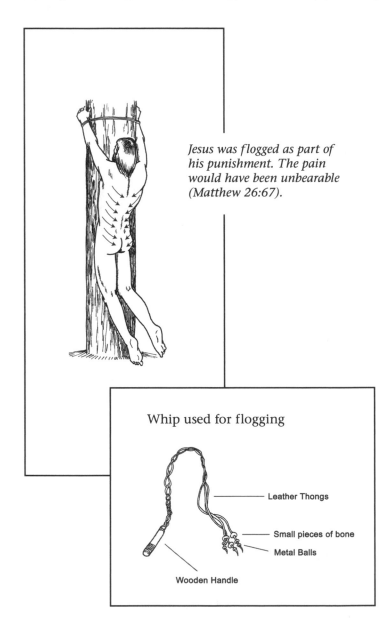

Jesus was flogged as part of his punishment. The pain would have been unbearable (Matthew 26:67).

Whip used for flogging

Leather Thongs

Small pieces of bone

Metal Balls

Wooden Handle

After being flogged, carrying the patibulum
was nearly impossible for Jesus.

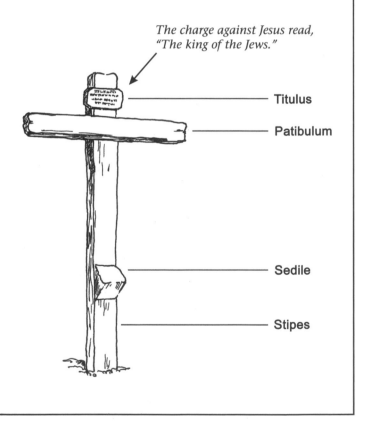

Crucifixion was so common in Jesus' time that the Romans had special names for the parts of the cross.

The charge against Jesus read, "The king of the Jews."

Titulus

Patibulum

Sedile

Stipes

Typical crucifixion involved being nailed to the cross through the wrists—an excruciatingly painful and humiliating punishment.

Median Nerve

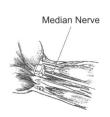

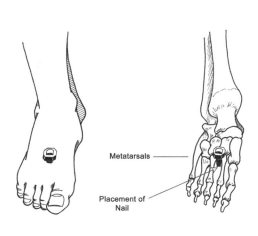

Metatarsals

Placement of Nail

During a crucifixion, a single nail usually was used to pin both feet together to the cross.

Eventually, the victim would be unable to lift himself to take a breath, and he would suffocate.

While the Romans broke the legs of the men who were crucified next to Jesus, they found that Jesus had already died. To make sure, they pierced his side with a spear, probably to puncture his heart (John 19:34)

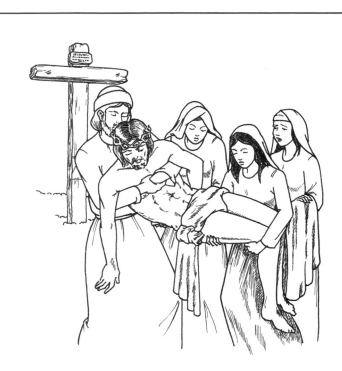

Joseph of Arimathea and several women took Jesus down and carried him to the tomb (Matthew 27:57–61).

The miracle of resurrection took place three days later, when Jesus rose from the dead.

COMPARATIVE RELIGIONS

Founder and date founded	Baha'i	Buddhism	Christianity
	Bahá'u'lláh (1817-1892) founded Babism in 1844 from which Baha'i grew.	Founded by Siddhartha Gautama (the Buddha) in Nepal in the 6th-5th centuries B.C.	Founded by Jesus of Nazareth, a Palestinian Jew, in the early 1st century A.D.
Number of adherents in 2000	About 7 million worldwide; 750,000 U.S.	360 million worldwide; 2 million U.S.	About 2 billion worldwide; 160 million U.S.
Main tenets	The oneness of God, the oneness of humanity, and the common foundation of all religion. Also, equality of men and women, universal education, world peace, and a world federal government.	Meditation and the practice of virtuous and moral behavior can lead to Nirvana, the state of enlightenment. Before that, one is subjected to repeated lifetimes, based on behavior.	Jesus is the Son of God and God in human form. In his death and resurrection, he redeems humanity from sin and gives believers eternal life. His teachings frame the godly life for his followers.
Sacred or primary writing	Bahá'u'lláh's teachings, along with those of the Bab, are collected and published.	The Buddha's teachings and wisdom are collected and published.	The Bible is a collection of Jewish and Near Eastern writings spanning some 1,400 years.

Confucianism	Hinduism	Islam	Judaism
Founded by the Chinese philosopher Confucius in the 6th-5th centuries B.C. One of several traditional Chinese religions.	Developed in the 2nd century B.C. from indigenous religions in India, and later combined with other religions, such as Vaishnavism.	Founded by the prophet Muhammad ca. A.D. 610. The word *Islam* is Arabic for "submission to God."	Founded by Abraham, Isaac, and Jacob ca. 2000 B.C.
6 million worldwide (does not include other traditional Chinese beliefs); U.S. uncertain.	900 million worldwide; 950,000 U.S.	1.3 billion worldwide; 5.6 million U.S.	14 million worldwide; 5.5 million U.S.
Confucius's followers wrote down his sayings or *Analects*. They stress relationships between individuals, families, and society based on proper behavior and sympathy.	Hinduism is based on a broad system of sects. The goal is release from repeated reincarnation through yoga, adherence to the Vedic scriptures, and devotion to a personal guru.	Followers worship Allah through the Five Pillars. Muslims who die believing in God, and that Muhammad is God's messenger, will enter Paradise.	Judaism holds the belief in a monotheistic God, whose Word is revealed in the Hebrew Bible, especially the Torah. Jews await the coming of a messiah to restore creation.
Confucius's *Analects* are collected and still published.	The Hindu scriptures and Vedic texts.	The Koran is a collection of Muhammad's writings.	The Hebrew scriptures compose the Christian Old Testament.

WORLD RELIGIONS

Listed by approximate number of adherents:

Christianity	2 billion
Islam	1.3 billion
Hinduism	900 million
Agnostic/Atheist/Non-Religious	850 million
Buddhism	360 million
Confucianism and Chinese traditional	225 million
Primal-indigenous	150 million
Shinto	108 million
African traditional	95 million
Sikhism	23 million
Juche	19 million
Judaism	14 million
Spiritism	14 million
Baha'i	7 million
Jainism	4 million
Cao Dai	3 million
Tenrikyo	2.4 million
Neo-Paganism	1 million
Unitarian-Universalism	800,000
Rastafarianism	700,000
Scientology	600,000
Zoroastrianism	150,000

U.S. CHRISTIAN DENOMINATIONS

Listed by approximate number of adult adherents:

Catholic	60 million
Baptist	30 million
Methodist/Wesleyan	13 million
Lutheran	9 million
Pentecostal/Charismatic	5 million
Orthodox	4 million
Presbyterian	4 million
Episcopal/Anglican	3 million
Churches of Christ	3 million
Congregational/United Church of Christ	2 million
Assemblies of God	1 million
Anabaptist	600,000
Adventist	100,000

PROVINCES OF THE ANGLICAN COMMUNION

- The Anglican Church in Aotearoa, New Zealand & Polynesia
- The Anglican Church of Australia
- The Church of Bangladesh
- Igreja Episcopal Anglicana do Brasil
- The Anglican Church of Burundi
- The Anglican Church of Canada
- The Church of the Province of Central Africa
- Iglesia Anglicana de la Region Central de America
- Province de L'Eglise Anglicane Du Congo
- The Church of England
- Hong Kong Sheng Kung Hui
- The Church of the Province of the Indian Ocean
- The Church of Ireland
- The Nippon Sei Ko Kai (The Anglican Communion in Japan)
- The Episcopal Church in Jerusalem & the Middle East
- The Anglican Church of Kenya
- The Anglican Church of Korea
- The Church of the Province of Melanesia
- La Iglesia Anglicana de Mexico
- The Church of the Province of Myanmar (Burma)
- The Church of Nigeria
- The Church of North India (United)
- The Church of Pakistan (United)
- The Anglican Church of Papua New Guinea
- The Episcopal Church in the Philippines

- L'Eglise Episcopal au Rwanda
- The Scottish Episcopal Church
- Church of the Province of South East Asia
- The Church of South India (United)
- The Church of the Province of Southern Africa
- Iglesia Anglicana del Cono Sur de America
- The Episcopal Church of the Sudan
- The Anglican Church of Tanzania
- The Church of the Province of Uganda
- The Episcopal Church
- The Church in Wales
- The Church of the Province of West Africa
- The Church in the Province of the West Indies

These Anglican churches are designated "Extra-Provincial," meaning they are not historically connected to a geographic province, as are other provinces of the Anglican Communion:

- The Church of Ceylon (Extra-Provincial to the Archbishop of Canterbury)
- Iglesia Episcopal de Cuba
- Bermuda (Extra-Provincial to Canterbury)
- The Lusitanian Church (Extra-Provincial to the Archbishop of Canterbury)
- The Reformed Episcopal Church of Spain (Extra-Provincial to the Archbishop of Canterbury)
- Falkland Islands (Extra-Provincial to Canterbury)

COMPARATIVE DENOMINATIONS:

	Anglican	Catholic	Orthodox
Founded when and by whom?	1534: Henry VIII is declared head of the Church of England. 1549: Thomas Cranmer produces the first *Book of Common Prayer*.	Catholics consider Jesus' disciple Peter (died ca. A.D. 66) the first pope. Through Gregory the Great (540-604), papacy is firmly established.	A.D 330: Emperor Constantine renames Byzantium "Constantinople" and declares Christianity the empire's religion.
Adherents in 2000?	45-75 million worldwide; about 3 million U.S.	About 1 billion worldwide; 60 million U.S.	About 225 million worldwide; about 4 million U.S.
How is Scripture viewed?	Protestant canon accepted. Scripture is interpreted in light of tradition and reason.	The canon is 46 books in the OT (Apocryhpha included) and 27 in the NT. Interpretation is subject to church tradition.	49 OT books (Catholic plus three more) and 27 NT. Scripture is subject to tradition.
How are we saved?	We share in Christ's victory, who died for our sins, freeing us through baptism to become living members of the church.	God infuses the gift of faith in the baptized, which is maintained by good works and receiving Penance and the Eucharist.	God became human so humans could be deified, that is, have the energy of God's life in them.
What is the church?	The body of Christ is based on "apostolic succession" of bishops, going back to the apostles. In the U.S., it is the Episcopal Church.	The mystical body of Christ, who established it with the pope as its head; he pronounces doctrine infallibly.	The body of Christ in unbroken historical connection with the apostles; the Roman pope is one of many patriarchs who govern.
What about the sacraments?	Baptism brings infant and convert initiates into the church; in Communion, Christ's body & blood are truly present.	Catholics hold seven sacraments. Baptism removes original sin; usually infants. The Eucharist undergoes transubstantiation.	Baptism initiates God's life in the baptized; adults and children. In the Eucharist, bread & wine are changed into body & blood.

Liturgical Churches

	Lutheran	Presbyterian	Methodist
Founded when and by whom?	1517: Martin Luther challenges Catholic teachings with his Ninety-five Theses. 1530: the Augsburg Confession is published.	1536: John Calvin writes *Institutes of the Christian Religion.* 1789: Presbyterian Church U.S.A. is organized.	1738: Anglican ministers John and Charles Wesley convert. 1784: U.S. Methodists form a separate church body.
Adherents in 2000?	About 60 million worldwide; about 9 million U.S.	40-48 million worldwide; 4 million U.S.	20-40 million worldwide; about 13 million U.S.
How is Scripture viewed?	Protestant canon contains 39 OT books, 27 NT. Scripture alone is the authoritative witness to the gospel.	Protestant canon accepted. Scripture is "witness without parallel" to Christ, but in human words reflecting beliefs of the time.	Protestant canon accepted. Scripture is primary source for Christian doctrine.
How are we saved?	We are saved by grace when God grants righteousness through faith alone. Good works inevitably result, but they are not the basis of salvation.	We are saved by grace alone. Good works result, but are not the basis of salvation.	We are saved by grace alone. Good works must result, but do not obtain salvation.
What is the church?	The congregation of believers, mixed with the lost, in which the gospel is preached and the sacraments are administered.	The body of Christ includes all of God's chosen and is represented by the visible church. Governed by regional "presbyteries" of elders.	The body of Christ, represented by church institutions. Bishops oversee regions and appoint pastors, who are itinerant.
What about the sacraments?	Baptism is necessary for salvation. The Lord's Supper is bread & wine that, with God's Word are truly Jesus' body & blood.	Baptism is not necessary for salvation. The Lord's Supper is Christ's body & blood, which are spiritually present to believers.	Baptism is a sign of regeneration; in the Lord's Supper, Jesus is really present.

COMPARATIVE DENOMINATIONS:

	Anabaptist	Congregational	Baptist
Founded when and by whom?	1523: Protestants in Zurich, Switzerland, begin believers' baptism. 1537: Menno Simons begins Mennonite movement.	1607: Members of England's illegal "house church" exiled. 1620: Congregationalists arrive in the New World on the *Mayflower*.	1612: John Smythe and other Puritans form the first Baptist church. 1639: The first Baptist church in America is established.
Adherents in 2000?	About 2 million worldwide; about 600,000 U.S.	More than 2 million worldwide; about 2 million U.S.	100 million worldwide; about 30 million U.S.
How is Scripture viewed?	Protestant canon accepted. Scripture is inspired but not infallible. Jesus is living Word; Scripture is written Word.	Protestant canon accepted. Bible is the authoritative witness to the Word of God.	Protestant canon accepted. Scripture is inspired and without error; the sole rule of faith.
How are we saved?	Salvation is a personal experience. Through faith in Jesus, we become at peace with God, moving us to follow Jesus' example by being peacemakers.	God promises forgiveness and grace to save "from sin and aimlessness" all who trust him, who accept his call to serve the whole human family.	Salvation is offered freely to all who accept Jesus as Saviour. There is no salvation apart from personal faith in Christ.
What is the church?	The body of Christ, the assembly and society of believers. No one system of government is recognized.	The people of God living as Jesus' disciples. Each local church is self-governing and chooses its own ministers.	The body of Christ; the redeemed throughout history. The term *church* usually refers to local congregations, which are autonomous.
What about the sacraments?	Baptism is for believers only. The Lord's Supper is a memorial of his death.	Congregations may practice infant baptism or believers' baptism or both. Sacraments are symbols.	Baptism is immersion of believers, only as a symbol. The Lord's Supper is symbolic.

Non-Liturgical Churches

	Churches of Christ	Adventist	Pentecostal
Founded when and by whom?	1801: Barton Stone holds Cane Ridge Revival in Kentucky. 1832: Stone's Christians unite with Disciples of Christ.	1844: William Miller's prediction of Christ's return that year failed. 1863: Seventh-Day Adventist Church is organized.	1901: Kansas college students speak in tongues. 1906: Azusa Street revival in L.A. launches movement. 1914: Assemblies of God organized.
Adherents in 2000?	5-6 million worldwide; about 3 million U.S.	About 11 million worldwide; about 100,000 U.S.	About 500 million worldwide; about 5 million U.S.
How is Scripture viewed?	Protestant canon accepted. Scripture is the Word of God. Disciples of Christ view it as a witness to Christ, but fallible.	Protestant canon accepted. Scripture is inspired and without error; Ellen G. White, an early leader, was a prophet.	Protestant canon accepted. Scripture is inspired and without error. Some leaders are considered prophets.
How are we saved?	We must hear the gospel, repent, confess Christ, and be baptized. Disciples of Christ: God saves people by grace.	We repent by believing in Christ as Example (in his life) and Substitute (by his death). Those who are found right with God will be saved.	We are saved by God's grace through Jesus, resulting in our being born again in the Spirit, as evidenced by a life of holiness.
What is the church?	The assembly of those who have responded rightly to the gospel; it must be called only by the name of Christ.	Includes all who believe in Christ. The last days are a time of apostasy, when a remnant keeps God's commandments faithfully.	The body of Christ, in which the Holy Spirit dwells; the agency for bringing the gospel of salvation to the whole world.
What about the sacraments?	Baptism is the immersion of believers only, as the initial act of obedience to the gospel. The Lord's Supper is a symbolic memorial.	Baptism is the immersion of believers only. Baptism and the Lord's Supper are symbolic only.	Baptism is immersion of believers only. A further "baptism in the Holy Spirit" is offered. Lord's Supper is symbolic.

FAMILY TREE OF CHRISTIANITY

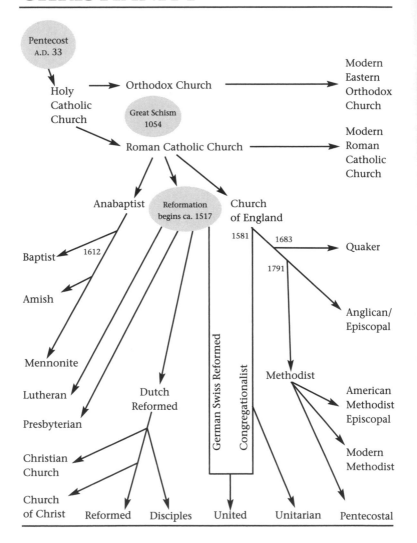

Pentecost A.D. 33

Holy Catholic Church

Great Schism 1054

Orthodox Church → Modern Eastern Orthodox Church

Roman Catholic Church → Modern Roman Catholic Church

Reformation begins ca. 1517

Anabaptist

Church of England

Baptist — 1612

Amish

Mennonite

Lutheran

Presbyterian

Dutch Reformed

Christian Church

Church of Christ

Reformed

Disciples

German Swiss Reformed

Congregationalist

United

1581

1683 → Quaker

1791

Anglican/ Episcopal

Methodist

American Methodist Episcopal

Modern Methodist

Unitarian

Pentecostal

GLOSSARY OF EPISCOPAL WORSHIP TERMS

acolyte: From the Greek for "to follow"; a lay liturgical assistant (often but not necessarily a youth) who serves in such various roles as crucifer, torchbearer, bannerbearer, bookbearer, candlelighter, and server.

Advent: From the Latin for "coming"; the four weeks before Christmas which constitute the first season of the liturgical year.

Advent wreath: A wreath with four candles, used during the four weeks of Advent.

alb: Full-length white vestment used in worship since the sixth century; usually worn with cincture. Worn by presiding and assisting ministers, acolytes, choristers.

altar: Table in the chancel used for the celebration of the Holy Communion. It is the central furnishing of the worship space.

altar rail: Railing enclosing the chancel at which people stand or kneel to receive Holy Communion.

ambo: Another (more historic) name for the pulpit, reading desk, or lectern.

antependium: Parament for pulpit and lectern.

apse: The semicircular (or polygonal) projection or alcove at the end of the chancel in traditional church architecture.

Ascension: Principal feast occurring 40 days after Easter Day, celebrating Christ's ascension to heaven.

ashes: Symbol of repentance and mortality used in the Ash Wednesday liturgy; made by burning palms from previous year.

Ash Wednesday: First day of Lent; occurs between February 4 and March 10. Name derives from the traditional practice of imposing ashes on worshipers' foreheads.

baptism: The sacrament of water and the Holy Spirit, in which we are joined to Christ's death and resurrection and initiated into the church.

Baptismal Covenant: Statements of belief and promises made by baptisands and/or their sponsors, and the entire assembly, during the service of baptism.

baptistery: The area in which the baptismal font is located.

Benedictus: (benn-eh-DIKtus) Latin title for the gospel canticle "Blessed be the God of Israel," in Morning Prayer, from Luke 1:68–79. Also refers to "Blessed is he who comes in the name of the Lord," in the Eucharist.

blue: Liturgical color for Advent in some churches; symbolizes hope.

burse: Square fabric-covered case in which the communion linens are often carried to and from the altar.

candlelighter: Long-handled device used to light and extinguish candles.

candlestick: Ornamental base holder for candle.

cassock: Full-length black "undergarment" worn under surplice or cotta.

catechumen: A person (usually an adult or older youth) preparing for Holy Baptism through a process of formation and special rites leading up to baptism, often at the Easter Vigil.

catechumenate: The process for preparing adults and older youth for Holy Baptism, often culminating at the Easter Vigil. It is a process of growth in spirituality, worship, service, as well as learning, and is based on the practice of the early church.

celebrant: The presiding cleric, whether bishop or priest, at the Eucharist, and, by extension, at other sacramental rites, such as baptism.

censer: Vessel in which incense is burned; also called thurible.

chalice: Cup used for the wine in the Holy Eucharist.

chancel: Elevated area where altar and, in some churches, pulpit/ambo are located.

chasuble: (CHAH-zuh-bel) The principal vestment for the Eucharistic liturgy; worn like a poncho by the priest or bishop over alb and stole.

chrism: (krizm) From the Greek for "Anointed One," a title for Christ. Fragrant oil used for anointing in Holy Baptism.

Christ the King: The last Sunday of the church year, celebrating the sovereignty of Christ.

Christmas: Principal feast of the church year which celebrates Christ's birth; also known as the Nativity of Our Lord.

ciborium: (sih-BOR-ee-um) Covered vessel which holds bread for the Holy Communion.

cincture: (SINK-chur) Rope belt worn with an alb.

columbarium: (KOLL-um- BARR-ee-um) Wall or other structure with niches for burial of ashes from cremation.

Compline: (KAHM-plin) From the Latin for "complete," referring to the prayers which complete the day's worship. An order for night prayer used as the last worship service before bed.

confirmation: A pastoral rite, quasi-sacramental in character, consisting of a reaffirmation of baptismal vows, with a blessing and the laying on of hands by a bishop.

cope: Long cape worn by worship leader, lay or ordained, for certain processions and ceremonial occasions.

corporal: Square white linen cloth placed on the center of the fair linen on the altar, on which the eucharistic vessels are placed for the celebration of Holy Communion.

corpus: Latin for "body." Carved figure of Christ attached to a cross; together, cross and corpus are a crucifix.

cotta: (KOTT-ah) Short white vestment worn over cassock by acolytes and choir members (unless albs are worn).

credence: (KREE-dentz) Shelf or table near the altar which holds sacramental vessels.

crosier: (KROH-zher) Crookshaped staff often carried by a bishop in his/her own diocese as a sign of shepherding authority.

crucifer: The acolyte who carries the processional cross.

crucifix: Cross with a corpus attached.

cruet: Glass vessel containing wine for the Holy Communion, oil for anointing, or water for the lavabo.

Daily Office: The daily services of readings and prayer, including Morning Prayer, Noonday Prayer, Evening Prayer, and Compline.

dalmatic: A vestment, rectangular in shape, with loose short sleeves, worn by a deacon at the Eucharist.

A cruet.

deacon: An order of the ordained ministry, charged particularly with a servant role in behalf of those in need, and to assist bishops and priests in the proclamation of the Gospel and the administration of the Sacraments.

dossal: Fabric hanging behind and above traditional east-wall altar.

east wall: The wall behind the altar, regardless of whether the wall is geographically to the east.

eastwall altar: An altar attached to the wall.

Easter: Principal feast of the church year which celebrates Christ's resurrection. Easter Day (which occurs between March 22 and April 25) is known as the Sunday of the Resurrection and as the "queen of feasts." The Easter season lasts for 50 days, a "week of weeks."

Easter Vigil: Festive liturgy on Easter Eve that includes the lighting of the new fire and procession of the paschal candle, readings from Scripture, Holy Baptism with the renewal of baptismal vows, and the first Eucharist of Easter.

elements: The earthly elements used in the celebration of the sacraments: bread and wine in Holy Communion, and water in Holy Baptism.

Epiphany: Principal feast celebrated on January 6, marking the visit of the magi to Jesus and the consequent revelation of Christ to the world.

eucharist: (YOO-kar-ist) From the Greek for "thanksgiving"; a name for the Holy Communion. The sacrament of Word, bread, and wine (in which the two earthly elements constitute the body and blood of our Lord) for which we give thanks, and through which we are nourished and strengthened in Christ's name and sustained in baptismal unity in him.

Evening Prayer: An evening worship service of scripture readings and prayer; also known as Vespers.

ewer: (YOO-er) A pitcher of water used at the baptismal font.

fair linen: Top white linen cloth covering the altar and thus serving as the table cloth for the Lord's Supper.

flagon: (FLAG-un) Pitcher-like vessel from which wine is poured into the chalice for the Holy Eucharist.

font: From the Latin for "fountain"; the pool or basin which holds water for Holy Baptism.

fraction: Ceremonial breaking of the bread in the Holy Communion liturgy.

free-standing altar: An altar which is not attached to the wall, and behind which the priest or bishop stands (facing the congregation) for the celebration of the Eucharist.

Fraction of the Bread in Holy Communion

frontal: Parament that covers the entire front of the altar, usually in a seasonal liturgical color; *see also* Laudian frontal.

funeral pall: Large cloth cover placed on the coffin when brought into the church for the burial liturgy. If an urn is used for ashes, a small cloth is used to cover it.

gold: Liturgical color for Easter Day, giving special prominence to this single most important feast of the year. White may also be used.

Good Friday: The Friday in Holy Week that observes Christ's crucifixion and death. The chancel and altar are bare of all appointments, paraments, and linens.

Greek cross: Ancient form of the cross in which the four arms are of equal length.

green: Liturgical color for the seasons after Epiphany and Pentecost; symbolic of growth in the Christian way of life.

Holy Trinity: The First Sunday after Pentecost, which celebrates the doctrine of the Trinity (one God in three persons: Father, Son, and Holy Spirit).

Holy Week: The week between the Sunday of the Passion (Palm Sunday) and Easter, which recalls the events of the last days of Christ's life.

host: Wafer, made of unleavened bread, for the Holy Eucharist.

incense: Mixture of resins for ceremonial burning, symbolic of our prayers rising to God (see Psalm 141); one of the gifts of the magi to Jesus on the Epiphany.

Incense.

intinction: From the Latin for "to dip"; the practice of receiving the eucharistic elements by dipping the host into the wine; does not work well with whole bread.

Laudian frontal: A type of frontal which entirely covers the top and all sides (to the floor) of a free-standing altar.

lavabo bowl: (lah-VAH-boh) Bowl used for the act of cleansing the celebrant's hands (this act is known as the lavabo) in the Eucharist or after the imposition of ashes or oil.

lectern: Reading stand from which the scripture readings may be proclaimed.

lectionary: The appointed system of scripture readings for the days of the church year. Also refers to the book that contains these readings.

lector: A lay assisting minister who reads the first and second readings from Scripture in the Eucharistic liturgy, or the biblical readings in other rites.

Lent: From the Anglo-Saxon for "spring"; the penitential 40-day season (excluding Sundays) before Easter, beginning with Ash Wednesday. Symbolic of Christ's 40 days in the wilderness. Lent is traditionally the season when candidates prepare for Holy Baptism, which is celebrated at the Easter Vigil.

lenten veil: Cloth used to cover crosses, sculpture, pictures, and other objects during Lent.

linens: Refers to three groups of white linen cloths: altar linens (cerecloth, protector linen, and fair linen), communion linens (corporal, pall, and purificators), and other linens (credence linen, offertory table linen, lavabo towel, and baptismal towel).

liturgy: From the Greek for "the people's work"; the prescribed worship services of the church.

Liturgy of the Word: That portion of the Eucharistic liturgy preceding the communion.

Magnificat: (mahg-NIFF-ihkaht) Latin title for the Song of Mary, "My soul proclaims the greatness of the Lord," which is the gospel canticle in Evening Prayer, and is from Luke 1:46–55.

Matins: (MAT-ins) From the Latin for "morning"; morning service of scripture reading and prayer; also known as Morning Prayer.

Maundy Thursday: (MAWN-dee) From the Latin mandatum for "commandment"; the Thursday in Holy Week which commemorates the institution of the Holy Communion at the Last Supper, during which Jesus commanded his disciples to love one another.

memorial garden: Usually a courtyard garden on church property in which ashes are mixed with the soil for interment after cremation.

miter: (MY-ter) From the Greek for "turban." A liturgical hat worn by a bishop.

Morning Prayer: Morning service of scripture reading and prayer; also known as Matins.

narthex: Entrance hall and gathering space of a church building which leads to the nave.

nave: From the Latin for "ship"; the section of the church building between the narthex and the chancel, where the congregation assembles for worship.

Miters go on top of bishops. They've been wearing them a long time.

new fire: The fire kindled on Easter Eve, used to light the paschal candle for the Easter Vigil. Symbolic of Christ's resurrected presence.

Nunc dimittis: (NOONK dih-MIH-tiss) Latin title for the Song of Simeon, the canticle from Luke 2:29–32, "Lord, you now have set your servant free," used in Evening Prayer and Compline.

ordinary: Those parts of the eucharistic liturgy which do not change from week to week.

orphrey: (OR-free) From the Latin for "gold." Ornamental band on a chasuble or parament.

pall: Linen-covered square placed over rim of the chalice. (*See also* funeral pall.)

Palm Sunday: *See* Sunday of the Passion.

paraments: Cloth hangings of various seasonal liturgical colors used to adorn the altar and pulpit/ambo/lectern.

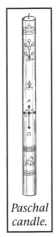

Paschal candle.

paschal candle: Large white candle carried in procession during the Easter Vigil, placed near the altar and lighted during the Easter season, symbolizing Christ's resurrected presence. At other times of the year, it is placed near the font and lighted for Holy Baptism, and placed at the head of the coffin and lighted for the burial liturgy.

passion red: The deep red liturgical color used in Holy Week. Symbolic of the blood of the passion of Christ.

paten: (PATT-en) Plate used to hold bread or hosts during the Eucharist.

pectoral cross: A cross on a chain, worn around the neck by a bishop.

Pentecost: From the Greek for "fiftieth day"; principal feast of the church year, occurring 50 days after Easter. Celebrates the descent of the Holy Spirit to the crowd gathered in Jerusalem.

Phos hilaron: (FOHS HILL-uhron) Greek for "light of glory"; hence, the Greek name for the canticle in Evening Prayer which begins "O gracious light."

piscina: A special drain in the sacristy which goes directly into the ground, used for disposal of water and wine remaining after the Holy Communion.

presider: The bishop or priest who leads the celebration of the Eucharist.

prie-dieu: (pree- DYOO) French term for "prayer desk"; used in the chancel for daily prayer services, confirmation, and weddings, as well as at other times when kneeling for prayer is desired.

priest: The second order of the ordained ministry of the Church. Also called a "presbyter."

processional cross: A cross or crucifix on a tall staff used to lead processions.

processional torch: *See* torch.

propers: The varying portions of the Eucharistic service which are appointed for each day (or season) of the church year; include the prayer of the day, psalm, readings, gospel acclamation, and proper preface.

pulpit: Raised reading desk in the chancel from which the gospel may be read and the sermon preached. *See also* ambo.

purificator: Square linen napkin used to cleanse the rim of the chalice during the distribution of Holy Communion.

purple: Liturgical color for Advent and Lent.

red: Liturgical color, symbolic of the fire of the Holy Spirit. Used on the Day of Pentecost, feasts of martyrs, and on other occasions.

reredos: (RAIR-eh-doss) Carved stone or wood panel behind and above an eastwall altar.

rite: The text and ceremonies of a worship service.

rubric: From the Latin for "red"; a direction for the proper conduct of a worship service. Rubrics are usually printed in red.

sacraments: Outward and visible signs of inward and spiritual grace, given by Christ, as sure and certain means by which we receive that grace, and as a pledge to assure us thereof.

sacristy: A room used for storage and preparation of items needed in worship; also used for vesting before services.

sanctuary lamp: A constantly burning candle sometimes suspended from the ceiling or mounted on the chancel wall; in Roman Catholic and some Episcopal churches, symbolizes the reserved sacrament.

sign of the cross: Gesture of tracing the outline of the cross with the hand, as a mark of belonging to Christ in Holy Baptism (during which it is first placed on one's forehead).

stole: Cloth band in liturgical color worn over the alb or surplice around a priest's neck and hanging to the knees. Signifies ordination and the yoke of obedience to Christ.

stripping of the altar: Ceremony at the conclusion of the Maundy Thursday liturgy, in which all appointments, linens, and paraments are removed from the altar and chancel in preparation for Good Friday.

Sunday of the Passion: The first day of Holy Week, also known as Palm Sunday. Commemorates both Christ's triumphant entry into Jerusalem and his crucifixion.

surplice: White vestment worn over the cassock; used especially for daily prayer services.

Te Deum laudamus: (tay DAY-um lau-DAH-moos) Latin for "We praise you, God"; a title for the canticle used in Morning Prayer.

Tenebrae: (TENN-eh-bray) From the Latin for "shadows"; a service sometimes used evenings during Holy Week, in which candles on a Tenebrae candle hearse are gradually extinguished.

thurible: Vessel in which incense is burned; also known as a censer.

thurifer: The person who carries the thurible.

torch: Large candle on a staff carried in processions, often flanking the processional cross or gospel book.

torchbearer: An acolyte who carries a processional torch.

Transfiguration: Feast celebrated on August 6, recalling Christ's transfiguration on the mountain.

Triduum: (TRIH-doo-um) Latin for "three days"; the three sacred days from Maundy Thursday evening through Easter Eve, which together celebrate the unity of the paschal mystery of Christ's death and resurrection.

veil: Cloth placed over sacramental vessels before and after the celebration of Holy Communion.

Torch.

versicles: Brief lines of scripture (often from the psalms) sung or said responsively in certain rites, including daily prayer.

Vespers: From the Latin for "evening"; an evening worship service of scripture readings and prayer. Also known as Evening Prayer.

vigil: A liturgical service on the eve of a feast, such as the Easter Vigil.

white: Liturgical color for Easter Day, giving special prominence to this single most important feast of the year. Gold may also be used.

EXTRA STUFF

THE BAPTISMAL COVENANT

Celebrant Do you believe in God the Father?
People I believe in God, the Father almighty,
    creator of heaven and earth.

Celebrant Do you believe in Jesus Christ, the Son of God?
People I believe in Jesus Christ, his only Son, our Lord.
    He was conceived by the power of the
      Holy Spirit and born of the Virgin Mary.
    He suffered under Pontius Pilate,
      was crucified, died, and was buried.
    He descended to the dead.
    On the third day he rose again.
    He ascended into heaven,
      and is seated at the right hand of the Father.
    He will come again to judge the living and
      the dead.

Celebrant Do you believe in God the Holy Spirit?
People I believe in the Holy Spirit,
    the holy catholic Church,
    the communion of saints,
    the forgiveness of sins,
    the resurrection of the body,
    and the life everlasting.

Celebrant Will you continue in the apostles' teaching and fellowship, in the breaking of bread, and in the prayers?
People I will, with God's help.

Celebrant Will you persevere in resisting evil, and, whenever you fall into sin, repent and return to the Lord?
People I will, with God's help.

Celebrant Will you proclaim by word and example the Good News of God in Christ?
People I will, with God's help.

Celebrant Will you seek and serve Christ in all persons, loving your neighbor as yourself?
People I will, with God's help.

Celebrant Will you strive for justice and peace among all people, and respect the dignity of every human being?
People I will, with God's help.

AN OUTLINE OF THE FAITH COMMONLY CALLED THE CATECHISM

(from The Book of Common Prayer, pages 845–862)

Human Nature

Q. What are we by nature?

A. We are part of God's creation, made in the image of God.

Q. What does it mean to be created in the image of God?

A. It means that we are free to make choices: to love, to create, to reason, and to live in harmony with creation and with God.

Q. Why then do we live apart from God and out of harmony with creation?

A. From the beginning, human beings have misused their freedom and made wrong choices.

Q. Why do we not use our freedom as we should?

A. Because we rebel against God, and we put ourselves in the place of God.

Q. What help is there for us?

A. Our help is in God.

Q. How did God first help us?

A. God first helped us by revealing himself and his will, through nature and history, through many seers and saints, and especially through the prophets of Israel.

God the Father

Q. What do we learn about God as creator from the revelation to Israel?

A. We learn that there is one God, the Father Almighty, creator of heaven and earth, of all that is, seen and unseen.

Q. What does this mean?

A. This means that the universe is good, that it is the work of a single loving God who creates, sustains, and directs it.

Q. What does this mean about our place in the universe?

A. It means that the world belongs to its creator; and that we are called to enjoy it and to care for it in accordance with God's purposes.

Q. What does this mean about human life?

A. It means that all people are worthy of respect and honor, because all are created in the image of God, and all can respond to the love of God.

Q. How was this revelation handed down to us?

A. This revelation was handed down to us through a community created by a covenant with God.

The Old Covenant

Q. What is meant by a covenant with God?

A. A covenant is a relationship initiated by God, to which a body of people responds in faith.

Q. What is the Old Covenant?

A. The Old Covenant is the one given by God to the Hebrew people.

Q. What did God promise them?
A. God promised that they would be his people to bring all the nations of the world to him.

Q. What response did God require from the chosen people?
A. God required the chosen people to be faithful; to love justice, to do mercy, and to walk humbly with their God.

Q. Where is this Old Covenant to be found?
A. The covenant with the Hebrew people is to be found in the books which we call the Old Testament.

Q. Where in the Old Testament is God's will for us shown most clearly?
A. God's will for us is shown most clearly in the Ten Commandments.

The Ten Commandments

Q. What are the Ten Commandments?
A. The Ten Commandments are the laws given to Moses and the people of Israel.

Q. What do we learn from these commandments?
A. We learn two things: our duty to God, and our duty to our neighbors.

Q. What is our duty to God?
A. Our duty is to believe and trust in God;

    I To love and obey God and to bring others to know him;

    II To put nothing in the place of God;

    III To show God respect in thought, word, and deed;

    IV And to set aside regular times for worship, prayer, and the study of God's ways.

Q. What is our duty to our neighbors?

A. Our duty to our neighbors is to love them as ourselves, and to do to other people as we wish them to do to us;

> V To love, honor, and help our parents and family; to honor those in authority, and to meet their just demands;

> VI To show respect for the life God has given us; to work and pray for peace; to bear no malice, prejudice, or hatred in our hearts; and to be kind to all the creatures of God;

> VII To use all our bodily desires as God intended;

> VIII To be honest and fair in our dealings; to seek justice, freedom, and the necessities of life for all people; and to use our talents and possessions as ones who must answer for them to God;

> IX To speak the truth, and not to mislead others by our silence;

> X To resist temptations to envy, greed, and jealousy; to rejoice in other people's gifts and graces; and to do our duty for the love of God, who has called us into fellowship with him.

Q. What is the purpose of the Ten Commandments?

A. The Ten Commandments were given to define our relationship with God and our neighbors.

Q. Since we do not fully obey them, are they useful at all?

A. Since we do not fully obey them, we see more clearly our sin and our need for redemption.

Sin and Redemption

Q. What is sin?

A. Sin is the seeking of our own will instead of the will of God, thus distorting our relationship with God, with other people, and with all creation.

Q. How does sin have power over us?

A. Sin has power over us because we lose our liberty when our relationship with God is distorted.

Q. What is redemption?

A. Redemption is the act of God which sets us free from the power of evil, sin, and death.

Q. How did God prepare us for redemption?

A. God sent the prophets to call us back to himself, to show us our need for redemption, and to announce the coming of the Messiah.

Q. What is meant by the Messiah?

A. The Messiah is one sent by God to free us from the power of sin, so that with the help of God we may live in harmony with God, within ourselves, with our neighbors, and with all creation.

Q. Who do we believe is the Messiah?

A. The Messiah, or Christ, is Jesus of Nazareth, the only Son of God.

God the Son

Q. What do we mean when we say that Jesus is the only Son of God?

A. We mean that Jesus is the only perfect image of the Father, and shows us the nature of God.

Q. What is the nature of God revealed in Jesus?
A. God is love.

Q. What do we mean when we say that Jesus was conceived by the power of the Holy Spirit and became incarnate from the Virgin Mary?
A. We mean that by God's own act, his divine Son received our human nature from the Virgin Mary, his mother.

Q. Why did he take our human nature?
A. The divine Son became human, so that in him human beings might be adopted as children of God, and be made heirs of God's kingdom.

Q. What is the great importance of Jesus' suffering and death?
A. By his obedience, even to suffering and death, Jesus made the offering which we could not make; in him we are freed from the power of sin and reconciled to God.

Q. What is the significance of Jesus' resurrection?
A. By his resurrection, Jesus overcame death and opened for us the way of eternal life.

Q. What do we mean when we say that he descended to the dead?
A. We mean that he went to the departed and offered them also the benefits of redemption.

Q. What do we mean when we say that he ascended into heaven and is seated at the right hand of the Father?
A. We mean that Jesus took our human nature into heaven where he now reigns with the Father and intercedes for us.

Q. How can we share in his victory over sin, suffering, and death ?
A. We share in his victory when we are baptized into the New Covenant and become living members of Christ.

The New Covenant

Q. What is the New Covenant?

A. The New Covenant is the new relationship with God given by Jesus Christ, the Messiah, to the apostles; and, through them, to all who believe in him.

Q. What did the Messiah promise in the New Covenant?

A. Christ promised to bring us into the kingdom of God and give us life in all its fullness.

Q. What response did Christ require?

A. Christ commanded us to believe in him and to keep his commandments.

Q. What are the commandments taught by Christ?

A. Christ taught us the Summary of the Law and gave us the New Commandment.

Q. What is the Summary of the Law?

A. You shall love the Lord your God with all your heart, with all your soul, and with all your mind. This is the first and the great commandment. And the second is like it: You shall love your neighbor as yourself.

Q. What is the New Commandment?

A. The New Commandment is that we love one another as Christ loved us.

Q. Where may we find what Christians believe about Christ?

A. What Christians believe about Christ is found in the Scriptures and summed up in the creeds.

The Creeds

Q. What are the creeds?

A. The creeds are statements of our basic beliefs about God.

Q. How many creeds does this Church use in its worship?

A. This Church uses two creeds: The Apostles' Creed and the Nicene Creed.

Q. What is the Apostles' Creed?

A. The Apostles' Creed is the ancient creed of Baptism; it is used in the Church's daily worship to recall our Baptismal Covenant.

Q. What is the Nicene Creed?

A. The Nicene Creed is the creed of the universal Church and is used at the Eucharist.

Q. What, then, is the Athanasian Creed?

A. The Athanasian Creed is an ancient document proclaiming the nature of the Incarnation and of God as Trinity.

Q. What is the Trinity?

A. The Trinity is one God: Father, Son, and Holy Spirit.

The Holy Spirit

Q. Who is the Holy Spirit?

A. The Holy Spirit is the Third Person of the Trinity, God at work in the world and in the Church even now.

Q. How is the Holy Spirit revealed in the Old Covenant?

A. The Holy Spirit is revealed in the Old Covenant as the giver of life, the One who spoke through the prophets.

Q. How is the Holy Spirit revealed in the New Covenant?
A. The Holy Spirit is revealed as the Lord who leads us into all truth and enables us to grow in the likeness of Christ.

Q. How do we recognize the presence of the Holy Spirit in our lives?
A. We recognize the presence of the Holy Spirit when we confess Jesus Christ as Lord and are brought into love and harmony with God, with ourselves, with our neighbors, and with all creation.

Q. How do we recognize the truths taught by the Holy Spirit?
A. We recognize truths to be taught by the Holy Spirit when they are in accord with the Scriptures.

The Holy Scriptures

Q. What are the Holy Scriptures?
A. The Holy Scriptures, commonly called the Bible, are the books of the Old and New Testaments; other books, called the Apocrypha, are often included in the Bible.

Q. What is the Old Testament?
A. The Old Testament consists of books written by the people of the Old Covenant, under the inspiration of the Holy Spirit, to show God at work in nature and history.

Q. What is the New Testament?
A. The New Testament consists of books written by the people of the New Covenant, under the inspiration of the Holy Spirit, to set forth the life and teachings of Jesus and to proclaim the Good News of the Kingdom for all people.

Q. What is the Apocrypha?

A. The Apocrypha is a collection of additional books written by people of the Old Covenant, and used in the Christian Church.

Q. Why do we call the Holy Scriptures the Word of God?

A. We call them the Word of God because God inspired their human authors and because God still speaks to us through the Bible.

Q. How do we understand the meaning of the Bible?

A. We understand the meaning of the Bible by the help of the Holy Spirit, who guides the Church in the true interpretation of the Scriptures.

The Church

Q. What is the Church?

A. The Church is the community of the New Covenant.

Q. How is the Church described in the Bible?

A. The Church is described as the Body of which Jesus Christ is the Head and of which all baptized persons are members. It is called the People of God, the New Israel, a holy nation, a royal priesthood, and the pillar and ground of truth.

Q. How is the Church described in the creeds?

A. The Church is described as one, holy, catholic, and apostolic.

Q. Why is the Church described as one?

A. The Church is one, because it is one Body, under one Head, our Lord Jesus Christ.

Q. Why is the Church described as holy?

A. The Church is holy, because the Holy Spirit dwells in it, consecrates its members, and guides them to do God's work.

Q. Why is the Church described as catholic?

A. The Church is catholic, because it proclaims the whole Faith to all people, to the end of time.

Q. Why is the Church described as apostolic?

A. The Church is apostolic, because it continues in the teaching and fellowship of the apostles and is sent to carry out Christ's mission to all people.

Q. What is the mission of the Church?

A. The mission of the Church is to restore all people to unity with God and each other in Christ.

Q. How does the Church pursue its mission?

A. The Church pursues its mission as it prays and worships, proclaims the Gospel, and promotes justice, peace, and love.

Q. Through whom does the Church carry out its mission?

A. The Church carries out its mission through the ministry of all its members.

The Ministry

Q. Who are the ministers of the Church?

A. The ministers of the Church are lay persons, bishops, priests, and deacons.

Q. What is the ministry of the laity?

A. The ministry of lay persons is to represent Christ and his Church; to bear witness to him wherever they may be and, according to the gifts given them, to carry on Christ's work of reconciliation in the world; and to take their place in the life, worship, and governance of the Church.

Q. What is the ministry of a bishop?

A. The ministry of a bishop is to represent Christ and his Church, particularly as apostle, chief priest, and pastor of a diocese; to guard the faith, unity, and discipline of the whole Church; to proclaim the Word of God; to act in Christ's name for the reconciliation of the world and the building up of the Church; and to ordain others to continue Christ's ministry.

Q. What is the ministry of a priest or presbyter?

A. The ministry of a priest is to represent Christ and his Church, particularly as pastor to the people; to share with the bishop in the overseeing of the Church; to proclaim the Gospel; to administer the sacraments; and to bless and declare pardon in the name of God.

Q. What is the ministry of a deacon?

A. The ministry of a deacon is to represent Christ and his Church, particularly as a servant of those in need; and to assist bishops and priests in the proclamation of the Gospel and the administration of the sacraments.

Q. What is the duty of all Christians?

A. The duty of all Christians is to follow Christ; to come together week by week for corporate worship; and to work, pray, and give for the spread of the kingdom of God.

Prayer and Worship

Q. What is prayer?

A. Prayer is responding to God, by thought and by deeds, with or without words.

Q. What is Christian Prayer?

A. Christian prayer is response to God the Father, through Jesus Christ, in the power of the Holy Spirit.

Q. What prayer did Christ teach us?

A. Our Lord gave us the example of prayer known as the Lord's Prayer.

Q. What are the principal kinds of prayer?

A. The principal kinds of prayer are adoration, praise, thanksgiving, penitence, oblation, intercession, and petition.

Q. What is adoration?

A. Adoration is the lifting up of the heart and mind to God, asking nothing but to enjoy God's presence.

Q. Why do we praise God?

A. We praise God, not to obtain anything, but because God's Being draws praise from us.

Q. For what do we offer thanksgiving?

A. Thanksgiving is offered to God for all the blessings of this life, for our redemption, and for whatever draws us closer to God.

Q. What is penitence?

A. In penitence, we confess our sins and make restitution where possible, with the intention to amend our lives.

Q. What is prayer of oblation?

A. Oblation is an offering of ourselves, our lives and labors, in union with Christ, for the purposes of God.

Q. What are intercession and petition?

A. Intercession brings before God the needs of others; in petition, we present our own needs, that God's will may be done.

Q. What is corporate worship?

A. In corporate worship, we unite ourselves with others to acknowledge the holiness of God, to hear God's Word, to offer prayer, and to celebrate the sacraments.

The Sacraments

Q. What are the sacraments?

A. The sacraments are outward and visible signs of inward and spiritual grace, given by Christ as sure and certain means by which we receive that grace.

Q. What is grace?

A. Grace is God's favor towards us, unearned and undeserved; by grace God forgives our sins, enlightens our minds, stirs our hearts, and strengthens our wills.

Q. What are the two great sacraments of the Gospel?

A. The two great sacraments given by Christ to his Church are Holy Baptism and the Holy Eucharist.

Holy Baptism

Q. What is Holy Baptism?

A. Holy Baptism is the sacrament by which God adopts us as his children and makes us members of Christ's Body, the Church, and inheritors of the kingdom of God.

Q. What is the outward and visible sign in Baptism?

A. The outward and visible sign in Baptism is water, in which the person is baptized in the Name of the Father, and of the Son, and of the Holy Spirit.

Q. What is the inward and spiritual grace in Baptism?

A. The inward and spiritual grace in Baptism is union with Christ in his death and resurrection, birth into God's family the Church, forgiveness of sins, and new life in the Holy Spirit.

Q. What is required of us at Baptism?

A. It is required that we renounce Satan, repent of our sins, and accept Jesus as our Lord and Savior.

Q. Why then are infants baptized?

A. Infants are baptized so that they can share citizenship in the Covenant, membership in Christ, and redemption by God.

Q. How are the promises for infants made and carried out?

A. Promises are made for them by their parents and sponsors, who guarantee that the infants will be brought up within the Church, to know Christ and be able to follow him.

The Holy Eucharist

Q. What is the Holy Eucharist?

A. The Holy Eucharist is the sacrament commanded by Christ for the continual remembrance of his life, death, and resurrection, until his coming again.

Q. Why is the Eucharist called a sacrifice?

A. Because the Eucharist, the Church's sacrifice of praise and thanksgiving, is the way by which the sacrifice of

Christ is made present, and in which he unites us to his one offering of himself.

Q. By what other names is this service known?

A. The Holy Eucharist is called the Lord's Supper, and Holy Communion; it is also known as the Divine Liturgy, the Mass, and the Great Offering.

Q. What is the outward and visible sign in the Eucharist?

A. The outward and visible sign in the Eucharist is bread and wine, given and received according to Christ's command.

Q. What is the inward and spiritual grace given in the Eucharist?

A. The inward and spiritual grace in the Holy Communion is the Body and Blood of Christ given to his people, and received by faith.

Q. What are the benefits which we receive in the Lord's Supper?

A. The benefits we receive are the forgiveness of our sins, the strengthening of our union with Christ and one another, and the foretaste of the heavenly banquet which is our nourishment in eternal life.

Q. What is required of us when we come to the Eucharist?

A. It is required that we should examine our lives, repent of our sins, and be in love and charity with all people.

Other Sacramental Rites

Q. What other sacramental rites evolved in the Church under the guidance of the Holy Spirit?

A. Other sacramental rites which evolved in the Church include confirmation, ordination, holy matrimony, reconciliation of a penitent, and unction.

Q. How do they differ from the two sacraments of the Gospel?

A. Although they are means of grace, they are not necessary for all persons in the same way that Baptism and the Eucharist are.

Q. What is Confirmation?

A. Confirmation is the rite in which we express a mature commitment to Christ, and receive strength from the Holy Spirit through prayer and the laying on of hands by a bishop.

Q. What is required of those to be confirmed?

A. It is required of those to be confirmed that they have been baptized, are sufficiently instructed in the Christian Faith, are penitent for their sins, and are ready to affirm their confession of Jesus Christ as Savior and Lord.

Q. What is Ordination?

A. Ordination is the rite in which God gives authority and the grace of the Holy Spirit to those being made bishops, priests, and deacons, through prayer and the laying on of hands by bishops.

Q. What is Holy Matrimony?

A. Holy Matrimony is Christian marriage, in which the woman and man enter into a life-long union, make their vows before God and the Church, and receive the grace and blessing of God to help them fulfill their vows.

Q. What is Reconciliation of a Penitent?

A. Reconciliation of a Penitent, or Penance, is the rite in which those who repent of their sins may confess them to God in the presence of a priest, and receive the assurance of pardon and the grace of absolution.

Q. What is Unction of the Sick?

A. Unction is the rite of anointing the sick with oil, or the laying on of hands, by which God's grace is given for the healing of spirit, mind, and body.

Q. Is God's activity limited to these rites?

A. God does not limit himself to these rites; they are patterns of countless ways by which God uses material things to reach out to us.

Q. How are the sacraments related to our Christian hope?

A. Sacraments sustain our present hope and anticipate its future fulfillment.

The Christian Hope

Q. What is the Christian hope?

A. The Christian hope is to live with confidence in newness and fullness of life, and to await the coming of Christ in glory, and the completion of God's purpose for the world.

Q. What do we mean by the coming of Christ in glory?

A. By the coming of Christ in glory, we mean that Christ will come, not in weakness but in power, and will make all things new.

Q. What do we mean by heaven and hell?

A. By heaven, we mean eternal life in our enjoyment of God; by hell, we mean eternal death in our rejection of God.

Q. Why do we pray for the dead?

A. We pray for them, because we still hold them in our love, and because we trust that in God's presence those who have chosen to serve him will grow in his love, until they see him as he is.

Q. What do we mean by the last judgment?
A. We believe that Christ will come in glory and judge the living and the dead.

Q. What do we mean by the resurrection of the body?
A. We mean that God will raise us from death in the fullness of our being, that we may live with Christ in the communion of the saints.

Q. What is the communion of saints?
A. The communion of saints is the whole family of God, the living and the dead, those whom we love and those whom we hurt, bound together in Christ by sacrament, prayer, and praise.

Q. What do we mean by everlasting life?
A. By everlasting life, we mean a new existence, in which we are united with all the people of God, in the joy of fully knowing and loving God and each other.

Q. What, then, is our assurance as Christians?
A. Our assurance as Christians is that nothing, not even death, shall separate us from the love of God which is in Christ Jesus our Lord. Amen.

THE TEN COMMANDMENTS
(from The Book of Common Prayer, page 350)

Hear the commandments of God to his people:
I am the Lord your God who brought you out of bondage.
You shall have no other gods but me.
Amen. Lord have mercy.

You shall not make for yourself any idol.
Amen. Lord have mercy.

You shall not invoke with malice the Name of the Lord
your God.
Amen. Lord have mercy.

Remember the Sabbath Day and keep it holy.
Amen. Lord have mercy.

Honor your father and your mother.
Amen. Lord have mercy.

You shall not commit murder.
Amen. Lord have mercy.

You shall not commit adultery.
Amen. Lord have mercy.

You shall not steal.
Amen. Lord have mercy.

You shall not be a false witness.
Amen. Lord have mercy.

You shall not covet anything that belongs to your neighbor.
Amen. Lord have mercy.

THE LORD'S PRAYER

(from The Book of Common Prayer, page 364)

Traditional

Our Father, who art in heaven,
hallowed be thy Name,
thy kingdom come,
thy will be done,
on earth as it is in heaven.
Give us this day our daily bread.
And forgive us our trespasses,
as we forgive those
who trespass against us.
And lead us not into temptation,
but deliver us from evil.
For thine is the kingdom,
and the power, and the glory,
for ever and ever. Amen.

Contemporary

Our Father in heaven,
hallowed be your Name,
your kingdom come,
your will be done,
on earth as in heaven.
Give us today our daily bread.
Forgive us our sins
as we forgive those
who sin against us.
Save us from the time of trial,
and deliver us from evil.
For the kingdom, the power,
and the glory are yours,
now and for ever. Amen.

DAILY DEVOTIONS FOR INDIVIDUALS AND FAMILIES

(from The Book of Common Prayer, pages 136–140)

These devotions follow the basic structure of the Daily Office of the Church.

When more than one person is present, the Reading and the Collect should be read by one person, and the other parts said in unison, or in some other convenient manner. (For suggestions about reading the Psalms, see page 582 of the BCP.)

For convenience, appropriate Psalms, Readings, and Collects are provided in each service. When desired, however, the Collect of the Day, or any of the Collects appointed in the Daily Offices, may be used instead.

The Psalms and Readings may be replaced by those appointed in

a) the Lectionary for Sundays, Holy Days, the Common of Saints, and Various Occasions, page 888 of the BCP.

b) the Daily Office Lectionary, page 934 of the BCP.

c) some other manual of devotion which provides daily selections for the Church Year.

In the Morning

From Psalm 51

Open my lips, O Lord, *
   and my mouth shall proclaim your praise.
Create in me a clean heart, O God, *
   and renew a right spirit within me.
Cast me not away from your presence *
   and take not your holy Spirit from me.
Give me the joy of your saving help again *
   and sustain me with your bountiful Spirit.
Glory to the Father, and to the Son, and to the Holy Spirit: *
   as it was in the beginning, is now, and will be for ever.
Amen.

A Reading

Blessed be the God and Father of our Lord Jesus Christ! By
his great mercy we have been born anew to a living hope
through the resurrection of Jesus Christ from the dead.
I Peter 1:3

A period of silence may follow.

A hymn or canticle may be used; the Apostles' Creed may be said.

Prayers may be offered for ourselves and others.

The Lord's Prayer

The Collect

Lord God, almighty and everlasting Father, you have brought
us in safety to this new day: Preserve us with your mighty
power, that we may not fall into sin, nor be overcome by
adversity; and in all we do, direct us to the fulfilling of your
purpose; through Jesus Christ our Lord. *Amen.*

At Noon

From Psalm 113

Give praise, you servants of the Lord; *
  praise the Name of the Lord.
Let the Name of the Lord be blessed, *
  from this time forth for evermore.
From the rising of the sun to its going down *
  let the Name of the Lord be praised.
The Lord is high above all nations, *
  and his glory above the heavens.

A Reading

O God, you will keep in perfect peace those whose minds are fixed on you; for in returning and rest we shall be saved; in quietness and trust shall be our strength. *Isaiah 26:3; 30:15*

Prayers may be offered for ourselves and others.

The Lord's Prayer

The Collect

Blessed Savior, at this hour you hung upon the cross, stretching out your loving arms: Grant that all the peoples of the earth may look to you and be saved; for your mercies' sake. *Amen.*

or this

Lord Jesus Christ, you said to your apostles, "Peace I give to you; my own peace I leave with you": Regard not our sins, but the faith of your Church, and give to us the peace and unity of that heavenly City, where with the Father and the Holy Spirit you live and reign, now and for ever. *Amen.*

In the Early Evening

This devotion may be used before or after the evening meal.

The Order of Worship for the Evening, page 109, may be used instead.

O gracious Light,
pure brightness of the everliving Father in heaven,
O Jesus Christ, holy and blessed!

Now as we come to the setting of the sun,
and our eyes behold the vesper light,
we sing your praises O God: Father, Son, and Holy Spirit.

You are worthy at all times to be praised by happy voices,
O Son of God, O Giver of life,
and to be glorified through all the worlds.

A Reading

It is not ourselves that we proclaim; we proclaim Christ Jesus
as Lord, and ourselves as your servants, for Jesus' sake. For
the same God who said, "Out of darkness let light shine,"
has caused his light to shine within us, to give the light of
revelation — the revelation of the glory of God in the face
of Jesus Christ. *2 Corinthians 4:5–6*

Prayers may be offered for ourselves and others.

The Lord's Prayer

The Collect

Lord Jesus, stay with us, for evening is at hand and the day
is past; be our companion in the way, kindle our hearts, and
awaken hope, that we may know you as you are revealed in
Scripture and the breaking of bread. Grant this for the sake
of your love. Amen.

At the Close of Day

Psalm 134

Behold now, bless the Lord, all you servants of the Lord, *
  you that stand by night in the house of the Lord.
Lift up your hands in the holy place and bless the Lord; *
  the Lord who made heaven and earth bless you out of Zion.

A Reading

Lord, you are in the midst of us and we are called by your
Name: Do not forsake us, O Lord our God. *Jeremiah 14:9, 22*

The following may be said

Lord, you now have set your servant free *
  to go in peace as you have promised;
For these eyes of mine have seen the Savior, *
  whom you have prepared for all the world to see:
A Light to enlighten the nations, *
  and the glory of your people Israel.

*Prayers for ourselves and others may follow. It is appropriate that prayers
of thanksgiving for the blessings of the day, and penitence for our sins,
be included.*

The Lord's Prayer

The Collect

Visit this place, O Lord, and drive far from it all snares of
the enemy; let your holy angels dwell with us to preserve us
in peace; and let your blessing be upon us always; through
Jesus Christ our Lord. *Amen.*

The almighty and merciful Lord, Father, Son, and Holy
Spirit, bless us and keep us. *Amen.*

BLESSINGS AT MEALS

(from The Book of Common Prayer, page 835)

Give us grateful hearts, our Father, for all thy mercies, and make us mindful of the needs of others; through Jesus Christ our Lord. *Amen.*

or this

Bless, O Lord, thy gifts to our use and us to thy service; for Christ's sake. *Amen.*

or this

Blessed are you, O Lord God, King of the Universe, for you give us food to sustain our lives and make our hearts glad; through Jesus Christ our Lord. *Amen.*

or this

For these and all his mercies, God's holy Name be blessed and praised; through Jesus Christ our Lord. *Amen.*